THE LAST FIGHT
— OF —
THE REVENGE

PETER EARLE

THE LAST FIGHT
— OF —
THE REVENGE

PETER EARLE

A JULIET GARDINER BOOK

COLLINS & BROWN

First published in Great Britain in 1992
by Collins & Brown Limited
Mercury House
195 Knightsbridge
London SW7 1RE

British Library Cataloguing-in-Publication Data.
A catalogue record for this book
is available from the British Library.

ISBN 1 85585 106 7

Typeset by Falcon Graphic Art, Wallington, Surrey
Printed and bound in Great Britain by The Bath Press

CONTENTS

LIST OF
ILLUSTRATIONS

INTRODUCTION

'I WONDER HOW many people have been inspired by this mad story, and how many battles have been actually won for England in the spirit thus engendered,' mused Robert Louis Stevenson on the story told in this book. It is the story of the most famous sea fight in English history in which Sir Richard Grenville with just one ship, the *Revenge*, fought an armada of fifty-three Spanish ships in the waters of Flores in the Azores.

The story has of course often been told before, most effectively perhaps by Sir Walter Raleigh in the same year as the events took place. Raleigh's pamphlet was the inspiration for Tennyson's rousing ballad of the 'Revenge' which was learned by heart by generations of British schoolchildren and still strikes a chord in our post-imperial world. 'Ship after ship, the whole night long, their high-built galleons came . . . ' More recently, the story has been retold in two biographies of Sir Richard Grenville published by A. L. Rowse and G. H. Bushnell in the 1930s, while details about the fight and the ship appear from time to time in such journals as the *Mariners' Mirror*.

I have two reasons for telling this story once again. First, because I was brought up on naval history and this story is just about the best and certainly the craziest in the long annals of England's maritime history. How could one ship fight fifty-three?

My second reason for writing the book is that I have more to tell about the fight and its background than any previous writer, since this account is the first one to make full use of the abundant source material in the archives at Simancas in Spain. A. L. Rowse, for instance, used just one Spanish document, the official relation of the fight. For this book, hundreds of Spanish documents have been consulted, enabling the Spanish point of view to be put much more clearly and adding many details to the description of the fight. No eyewitness account of the battle by an English observer has survived, so this Spanish testimony is vital if the last fight of the *Revenge* is to be taken out of the realm of myth and seen for the very real event that it was.

Most of the book focuses directly on the events leading up to the fight and on the fight itself. It has however been my intention to use that focus to paint a broader picture of the maritime world of the period and so give the reader the feel of life at sea and the nature of naval warfare in the last decade of the sixteenth century. The book then is about the sea and ships, though the land on which sailors depend will get its due mention. We will visit London and Ferrol, Lisbon and Havana and, above all, we will visit 'Flores in the Azores where Sir Richard Grenville lay', that island in the mid-Atlantic whose mighty cliffs looked on impassively as the *Revenge* fought her last fight.

Translations from the Spanish, and occasionally Portuguese, are by myself unless otherwise noted and are not always completely literal. I have tried instead to make quotations readable while retaining the sense of the original. Dates are Old Style which means that, from a Spanish point of view, everything happened ten days later than appears in the text, an adjustment which sometimes means that saints' days are misdated.

My thanks are due to Richard King and Fathom-Line Ltd who provided valuable assistance in the early stages of research, to Juliet Gardiner who read the book in draft and to Mina Moshkeri who drew the maps. Finally, I must thank my friend and colleague David Hebb for sharing with me his knowledge of the maritime world of the late sixteenth century, for his constant encouragement and for a very impressive editing job on the final draft.

London, September 1991   PETER EARLE

CHAPTER ONE

A PROVIDENTIAL VICTORY

Almost all Spain was covered in mourning . . .
and there were tears and sighs everywhere.[1]

THE KNIGHTS WERE jousting before their queen. Her favourite, the Earl of Essex, ran two tilts against the Earl of Cumberland, corsair as well as jouster and soon to become the Queen's Champion. 'Several other gentlemen then joined; and they tilted two against two; and then four against four . . . It was a beautiful sight.' The Elizabethans loved chivalry and heroic display and there were many such scenes of courtly violence in the late summer and autumn of 1588, as knights and lords prepared for the annual climax of the jousting season on 17 November, the anniversary of Queen Elizabeth's accession to the throne.[2]

Queen's Day had developed quite spontaneously as a day of Protestant celebration with jousting just one of many attractions. Sermons praised the Queen for deliverance of the country from the yoke of Catholicism. Stately processions wound their way through cities and towns and even the smallest villages honoured their queen. Psalms were sung and bells rung, while oxen and venison roasted on great bonfires. Nowhere was the day celebrated with more zest than at sea. Thomas Cavendish had astonished the Spaniards in a remote port of South America when he celebrated Queen's Day in 1587 with a discharge of his guns and a magnificent firework display. A year later, he enhanced the celebrations in London with a display of booty plundered in the Spanish Pacific from 'one of the richest vessels that ever sailed the seas', evidence of the long reach of English maritime power much appreciated by the Queen as she watched the spectacle from Greenwich.[3]

Queen's Day can never have been observed with more devotion and cheer than in 1588 as the nation gave thanks for delivery from the most terrible Catholic threat of all — the Spanish Armada. It had been a great deliverance. All Europe had waited to learn the fate of what the Spaniards called the Enterprise of England, an enterprise which King Philip of Spain had personally dedicated to God. Catholic Europe had celebrated prematurely at the news that a great victory had been won, scores of English ships sunk and the arch-pirate, Sir Francis Drake, dead or held a prisoner. Even the English captains were still not sure whether they had won as they turned for home, victuals and ammunition spent, after watching the mighty ships of the Armada sail northward past the Firth of Forth. But slowly, the scale of the terrible Spanish disaster began to sink in.

At least a third of the 130 ships assembled for the Armada from all over Europe were lost and the true figure may well be nearer a half.[4] One ship was abandoned to the English after an explosion in its powder magazine; another was captured after an accidental collision. A few ships were run aground after being holed by English gunfire in the great fight off the banks of Flanders, or as a result of cutting their anchor cables in panic at the approach of English fireships. But only one ship was actually sunk at sea as a result of being battered by the English guns. These guns did however weaken several other ships and so made them more vulnerable to the tempests and heavy seas which struck the Armada as it sailed into the North Atlantic.

The Armada was now scattered by the gale-force winds, many of the ships a wretched sight with yards and masts lost and sails in tatters as they approached the west coast of Ireland, an area they had been warned to avoid at all costs and for which they had no charts. The local Irish and their English masters observed the gale with glee, 'a most extreme wind and cruel storm . . . which put us in very good hope that many of the ships should be beaten up and cast away upon the rocks.' And so it happened. The coasts and offshore islands of Ireland were littered with wrecks, at Doonbeg on the coast of Clare, in Scattery Roads, on Streedagh Strand and Mutton Island, in Blasket Sound and the Bay of Tralee and in a host of other places whose names alone sound murderous in Castilian.

Some ships succumbed even after making it back to Spain. One blew up; others ran ashore for lack of anchors or of men to lower them and work the sails. And those that finally reached their moorings safely were pitiable to behold, 'broken and distressed, without rigging, sails or cables'. The Duke of Medina Sidonia, reluctant commander of this miserable Armada, felt unable to describe to the King 'the misfortunes and miseries that have befallen us, because they are the worst that have been known on any voyage'.

The losses of men were equally appalling, maybe half of the 30,000 polyglot soldiers and sailors who had been confessed and blessed, one by one, as they waited to leave Corunna harbour. Only a small minority of these were killed in battle. Many died of epidemic diseases, weakened by thirst and starvation in a fleet desperately short of wholesome food and water. And many more were drowned as their ships wrecked on the Irish coast or as they tried to swim or wade to the safety of the shore, an illusory safety since many survivors were massacred by the Irish and even more were slaughtered on the orders of the English. Many of those who did return to the shores of Spain were only half alive and thousands more were to die soon after arrival.

Spain was heartbroken. 'A terrible shame, worthy to be wept over all one's life,' wrote a monk of El Escorial. 'To see the flower of Spain lost without anything of consideration or worthy of memory having been done.'[5] No one was more desolate than the man who had sent the Armada to sea, Philip II the Prudent, who sat at his desk in this same monastery-palace of El Escorial poring over the reports that slowly brought home the truth of the extent of his losses. At first the King despaired so much that he hoped to die, 'so as not to see so much ill fortune and disgrace'. But such dejection was expressed in private. Philip's public face was one of amazing stoicism. 'The Spanish King himself bare the overthrow very patiently, as received from God,' wrote the contemporary chronicler, William Camden. 'He gave, and commanded to be given all over Spain, thanks to God and the Saints that it was no greater; and shewed singular pity and commiseration in relieving the distressed souldiers and mariners.'[6]

God's providence in sending storms to destroy the Armada was interpreted differently by the English and the Spaniards and, by extension, by

Protestant and Catholic Europe. Both sides were agreed, however, that it was not men who had defeated the Spaniards. 'Everybody died, not at the hands of enemies, but of the storms and waves of the sea,' as a Spaniard put it. 'We were onely delivered by His owne gracious providence,' wrote the English chronicler John Speed, 'and not by any policy or power of our owne.' The English guns had been more terrible than anything previously encountered at sea, as the *'gran furia de artilleria'* pounded away hour after hour, but they had sent only one Spanish ship to the bottom. The plain fact was that, for all their vaunted gunnery and skills at sea, the English had been unable to prevent a fleet which seemed 'sufficient to lay waste the whole world' from sailing right into the Straits of Dover.[7]

Thereafter, things had of course gone seriously wrong. But, despite this, the final lesson learned by King Philip was not one of despair. New ships could be built, more men found and the Enterprise of England could still be achieved. The sick and ageing king withdrew even further from the world, devoted himself even more to prayer and annotation of the flood of letters and reports that ever so slowly set in motion that huge bureaucracy that was the Spanish Empire; but he did not forget England. The war went on.

This war clearly had much to do with religion. It was after all a war in which the Catholic King of Spain endeavoured to invade England and restore the heretic island to the true faith. And it was a war in which Protestant Englishmen under the inspiring but often hesitant leadership of their queen sought to prevent the King of Spain from achieving this ambition. Religious hatred is a powerful emotion and it was constantly stoked by priests and propagandists of both sides. English men and women absorbed as children and retained as adults a vivid memory of what Catholicism meant — the racks, thumbscrews and dungeons of the Spanish Inquisition and the fires of Smithfield where Protestant martyrs had been burned to death for their faith in the quite recent days of Queen Mary's reign. But religion alone is not sufficient to explain the great war between England and Spain which lasted from 1585 to 1604. By no means all the Queen's subjects were true Protestants. Many remained Catholics, either openly or secretly, while many more, probably the majority, were ready to worship as their rulers directed.

Lack of religious fervour did not however lead to indifference when England was threatened with invasion by Spain.

Such patriotism was actively encouraged by poets and teachers, parsons and artists who combined to create an image of England which could be admired and, if necessary, defended. The English had long learned to despise foreigners, but that sense of destiny, of a God-given right to rampage through the world, is largely a product, and a conscious product, of the age of Elizabeth. And it was of course the Queen, whose image was promoted in paintings and poetry, in progresses, processions and the cult of Queen's Day, who was the personification of this militant England. There is not much of religion in such paintings of Elizabeth as the 'Armada portrait' attributed to George Gower. Here, we do not see the Queen on her knees giving thanks to God for the delivery of her country. She rises, magnificently and triumphantly, between two windows through which the arrival and the defeat of the Spanish Armada are portrayed. And her right hand rests, lightly but with a sense of ownership, on a globe.[8]

But this was just propaganda. The Queen did not love war and did not have sufficient money or men or even the desire to conquer the world. She only went to war in 1585, with great reluctance, when she feared that the revolt of the Dutch against their former Spanish masters was about to collapse. A resurgent Spain in control of the ports of Holland, Zeeland and Flanders, in possession of Dutch ships, money and resources, was too dangerous to contemplate. An expeditionary force was sent to fight in the Netherlands and Francis Drake and other sea-dogs were let loose to pillage the Spanish Empire. Only when the Queen took these steps did King Philip think seriously about invading England. The heretic English had always been an embarrassment to the devout king who had once been married to their Catholic Queen Mary. They now became a nuisance as well in the Netherlands, an area where Spanish pride and sense of possession had been seriously challenged. They were to become more than a nuisance in that wider world of the Spanish Empire whose cities, ships, goods and men were so savagely plundered by English corsairs. Worse still, these corsairs threatened the King of Spain's financial lifeline, the imports of treasure from America. The Enterprise of England became a necessity.

English soldiers were to remain in the Netherlands during Elizabeth's war and were soon to be in northern France as well, propping up the armies of the Protestant Henry of Navarre who came to the French throne as Henry IV in 1589 and attempting to dislodge the Spaniards from what appeared to be some very dangerous launching-pads for invasion in Brittany and Normandy. These expeditions were in no sense holy wars; they were part of a successful strategy to prevent a Spanish invasion by supporting as cheaply as possible anyone else who was opposed to the Spaniards. That such people were often Protestants was important and a reflection of the current state of Europe. But religion was not the only factor determining allegiance. Protestant England was quite happy to spend scarce money and send men to support Dom Antonio of Crato, a rival claimant to Philip II for the throne of Portugal, a man as staunchly Catholic as anyone in Spain, as indeed were those Portuguese who followed him.

Such expeditions and the foreign policy that gave rise to them serve to remind us that Elizabeth's war was not fought just, or even mainly, at sea. It is however the war at sea which is the subject of this book and it will be useful to close this chapter by considering the resources with which it was fought. Contemporaries were agreed that the professional soldiers in the armies of Spain were the finest in the world, but man for man and ship for ship the English were generally thought to be the masters at sea. The spreading horizons of English international trade had created a large pool of skilled and experienced deep-sea sailors, while two decades of piracy and privateering had honed the fighting skills of England's mariners. Privateers, private men of war, or 'corsairs' as they were known in most other European languages, were a respectable sort of pirate who bore a licence to attack and plunder the enemies of their country. Such service was attractive to sailors and could be very profitable, so that it was only with great difficulty that English sailors could be induced or forced to serve in the Queen's fine ships.

This navy consisted of some forty ships of which about two dozen formed the main battle fleet,[9] the rest being smaller ships which played an auxiliary role. Such numbers could be rapidly increased by calling on privateers or large armed merchantmen, as was done in Armada year, but it was the Queen's ships which formed the fighting core of the fleet. These were without doubt the finest ships of war in the world, the product of some thirty years of experiment and innovation in naval shipbuilding.

The most important change had been a gradual reduction in the number of the largest class of ship of 1,000 tons or more, the 'high-charged' ships whose towering forecastles and poops are so familiar from paintings of the Spanish Armada. England still had some of these floating fortresses, but they were being increasingly replaced by what were known as 'race-built' galleons. These were medium-sized galleons of about 500 tons, long and lean in comparison with their clumsy predecessors, with a ratio of keel length to beam of about three to one. The towering poops were replaced by a series of decks stepped down into the waist of the galleon and the forecastle was also severely cut down. The result was a ship which 'lay low and snug in the water', faster, handier and able to sail closer to the wind.[10]

Such improvements did not satisfy everyone. Many preferred the high-charged ships 'for majesty and terror of the enemy', a preference reinforced by the Armada campaign when everyone had seen for themselves just how majestic and terrible the great Spanish galleons were. Reduction of the superstructure also meant there was much less covered space, leaving what was left grossly overcrowded with men, victuals and stores. The new galleons were also thought difficult to defend once they had been boarded, in the absence of the great castles in which men could work the ship and fire down on boarders. But, even after the Armada, this seemed largely an academic problem since none of the Queen's ships had ever been boarded by the enemy.

This was partly because the English ships were faster and nimbler than those of Spain and could therefore get themselves out of trouble. It was also and principally because of their guns and the skills of their gunners which were the envy of Europe. The weight of the guns on the larger English ships was some eight to ten per cent of their tonnage, over twice the relative weight of the guns on Spanish ships. The individual pieces were also better cast and were mounted on easy-to-handle and compact truck carriages, as opposed to the clumsy mountings borrowed from field artillery which continued to be used by all other navies into the seventeenth century. This meant that the English guns were easier to reload and their rate of fire was much higher than could be attained by Spanish gunners, an advantage which had been clearly seen in the great gun battle off the banks of Flanders during the Armada campaign.[11]

English superiority in naval guns and gunnery has led historians to make striking contrasts between English and Spanish tactics at sea. The Spaniards are often derided for what is seen as the medieval tactics of closing quickly with the enemy, firing their guns just once as they came in and then boarding in the smoke and confusion. Once aboard their enemy, the professional skills of the large number of soldiers carried on Spanish ships would soon carry the day. The English, on the other hand, are seen to have invented the modern way of naval warfare in which the object is to stand off from the enemy and batter him with one's guns until he surrenders or sinks. There is something in this contrast, but it exaggerates the differences between the navies of the two nations and also tends to overestimate the destructive power of the English guns, good though they were.

The English were in fact just as keen to take a ship by boarding as their enemies, indeed, probably even more so, since nearly all successful English sailors had their origins in piracy or privateering and no pirate or privateer wants to sink an enemy ship and thus see all his profit go to the bottom. So the main objective in fighting at sea, for Englishman and Spaniard alike, was to board and capture ships, preferably still seaworthy and intact, so that they could be profitably plundered and sold as a prize. England's dominance in guns and gunnery, however, gave her sailors the chance to determine the nature of the battles they fought. Against a strong enemy, as in the Armada campaign, the English could stand back and check any attack with their devastating cannon fire. Whether the enemy was equal in strength or weaker, the superior gunnery of the English enabled them to close and board at will.

War at sea did not end with the destruction of the Armada. This book will examine and attempt to illuminate the post-Armada phase of the war by looking in detail at one exciting episode which resulted in a rare Spanish victory in a battle at sea. It was no ordinary battle and no ordinary victory. Sir Francis Bacon described it as memorable 'even beyond credit, and to the height of some heroical fable', while the victorious Spaniards were so sad that they did not 'sing *Te Deums* about the streets neither make bonfires as they were wont of their victories, but are as still as a nest of young birds'.[12] What sort of victory was that?

CHAPTER TWO

AFTER THE ARMADA

Whosoever commands the sea commands the trade;
whosoever commands the trade of the world
commands the riches of the world
and consequently the world itself.[1]

As ENGLAND CELEBRATED in the autumn of 1588, many thought the time had come to finish the war with Spain once and for all. The English had not lost a single ship in the actions in the Channel, nor in the great gun battle off the banks of Flanders, nor in the terrible storms which shattered the Spanish Armada. Surely now was the time to send forth the fleet to destroy what remained of the Spanish ships as they lay helpless at their moorings in Lisbon and the ports of northern Spain and so remove for ever, or at least for many years, the threat of Spanish sea power.

Such a policy was however merely wishful thinking, since neither ships nor men were fit to sail after six months' service at sea. All the ships were in poor condition, some damaged by the Spanish cannon, most of them leaking, foul inside and out, ropes, sails and yards in need of repair or replacement. As for the men, they were in even worse condition, consuming rotten victuals or none at all and dying by the thousand from shipboard epidemics. As Lord Admiral Howard of Effingham, the commander-in-chief, observed with aristocratic sadness, 'it would grieve any man's heart to see them that have served so valiantly to die so miserably.'[2]

Even if England's ships and sailors had been in perfect health, there was no money to pay them to fight any more, for the defence against the Armada had completely drained the exchequer which paid out an unprecedented £400,000 in the year ending Michaelmas 1588. The autumn saw undignified scenes as ships were laid up and soldiers and sailors paid off as quickly as possible. The sick were left untended and indeed encouraged to die so as to save the exchequer money, a sad contrast to the care and attention which Crown, Church and people were devoting to the survivors of the Armada in Spain.

The English rarely treated those who served in their wars with generosity and there was nothing unusual about this callous neglect. No one doubted that there would be more men to serve, willingly or not, in some great stroke against Spain in the spring when the ships would once again be ready to sail. Much more of a problem was how to finance such a campaign, for the taxpayers seemed reluctant to support their patriotism with a further call on their purses. The solution to this problem was typical of this age of plunder. The great expedition of 1589, the Counter-Armada as it is often called, would be financed on a joint-stock basis with the Queen as only one of many shareholders eager to fill their purses at the expense of Spain. When it was learned that the expedition was to be jointly commanded by England's most experienced soldier and most successful sailor — Sir John Norris and Sir Francis Drake — the money and the volunteers came rolling in. A huge force of six Queen's ships, over 100 private ships and more than 20,000 soldiers and sailors was eventually gathered together, numbers which bear comparison with those of the Spanish Armada itself, an instructive illustration of the power of the profit motive in war.

The aims of this mighty armada had swollen during the winter and, by 18 April 1589, when the fleet left Plymouth after numerous delays, there were three main objectives.[3] The fleet was first to destroy the remnants of the Spanish Armada which were refitting in the ports of northern Spain, particularly in Santander where there were said to be forty or fifty ships. This job done, the English were to sail to Portugal, capture Lisbon and establish the pretender Dom Antonio on the Portuguese throne, a task thought to be simplicity itself since the Portuguese were only waiting for Dom Antonio's arrival to rise in revolt against their Spanish masters. And finally, with the Spanish fleet destroyed and Portugal and the Portuguese Empire laid open for exploitation by English merchants, the victorious English fleet was to sail to the Azores, capture the incoming treasure galleons and take one or all the islands as a mid-Atlantic base for further attacks on Spanish merchant shipping. It seems probable that it was this last objective which was most attractive, both to those who backed the Counter-Armada and to those who took part in it, for the capture of the Spanish treasure fleets coming from America was something which gripped the English imagination throughout the war. This is hardly surprising for the feat always seemed possible and the potential rewards were staggering. The 1587 treasure fleet, for instance, had carried bullion and coin belonging to the Spanish Crown and individuals worth £3,500,000, nearly nine times the expenditure of the English government in Armada year.

Needless to say, not one of these ambitious objectives was achieved. The Counter-Armada seemed doomed to disaster and disappointment from the start with its divided command, the inevitable conflict between strategic aims and profit and its multiplicity of aims. Using the excuse of contrary winds, Drake refused to sail to Santander which was inconveniently placed as a stopping point on a voyage to Lisbon. Instead, he raided Corunna where there was not much Spanish shipping to destroy, though there was plenty of wine to drink and many of the men were still drunk or weakened by alcoholic abuse when they landed in Portugal. The catalogue of disasters continued. The Portuguese did not rise for Dom Antonio; the English had brought no siege train to batter down the walls of Lisbon; Drake, who sailed to the mouth of the Tagus, did not manage to link up with Norris, who marched his sick and inebriated army across country from the fishing port of Peniche to the suburbs of Lisbon where they wilted under the summer sun. The Earl of Essex, who had infuriated the Queen by running away to join in the expedition without her permission, knocked on the gates of Lisbon, but that was as far as he could go without a siege train. In June, Drake and Norris, now reunited, gave up and sailed for the Azores, but were prevented by storms from even reaching the islands, let alone capturing them or the treasure fleet. And so they sailed home with nothing achieved, the investors £100,000 poorer, the ships damaged by storm and 10,000 men dead or nearly dead, many dying under the Portuguese sun and many more from those shipboard diseases which so regularly struck the great fleets of the period. The Spaniards had no monopoly on disaster.

Drake took the blame for the failure of the Counter-Armada and was given no further command at sea until his final fatal voyage to the West

Indies in 1595. Failure also meant that there was now little support for those amphibious naval operations on the grand scale for which Drake had been one of the greatest advocates. It was time to rethink both naval and military strategy. Spanish failure in 1588 and English failure in 1589 meant that the war was likely to go on for a long time, until Spain grew so tired of her ambition to curb the insolent and heretical English that she sued for peace. What was the best and most economical way to achieve this end?

By the autumn of 1589, when Drake's ships limped home from their disastrous expedition, the strategic situation had changed quite considerably. The galleons of Spain which had earlier been described as lying in the ports of Santander and San Sebastian, 'all unrigged and their ordnance on the shore', were no longer such passive targets for destruction by a determined English raiding force. Early in June, Francisco de Molina had reported to King Philip from Santander that there were fifty ships there and in the port of Pasajes which could be got ready for sea. He proposed a *jornada* to fill them with 10,000 soldiers and capture the port of Milford Haven.[4] Nothing came of this nor of other similar ambitious proposals but, by July, several ships had been repaired sufficiently to set sail for the naval base at Corunna which Drake and Norris had found so empty of warships in April and May. Less than a year after the disaster of the Armada, the Spaniards had the makings of a seagoing fleet once more, a fact which made the Queen and her advisers once again fearful of invasion and so unwilling to commit too many of the Queen's ships outside the English Channel.

There had been important changes too in the complex three-cornered civil war going on in France. Here, English policy centred on the need to prevent the Catholic League, supported by Spain, from becoming too powerful and, in particular, from becoming too powerful in northern France and the Channel ports. In July 1589, the kaleidoscope of French politics was shaken up by the assassination of the King, Henry III, and his succession by Henry of Navarre as Henry IV. Henry of Navarre was a Protestant and England's ally, but the immediate result of his accession to the throne was to create a military crisis in northern France. This demanded the dispatch of English money and men to prop up the armies of the new king and so prevent much of France from falling under Spanish hegemony. Such fears were heightened by continuous rumours, which late in 1590 were to become reality, that the Spaniards planned to send an expeditionary force to occupy one or more of the ports of Brittany. The thought of a revitalized Spanish navy and large numbers of Spanish soldiers in, for instance, Brest or St Malo at the windward end of the Channel made the Queen still more determined to keep most of her navy close to home.

Such considerations meant that for the rest of 1589 and for the next few years the English would eschew grand overseas expeditions to Spain, the West Indies or Portugal, such campaigns having in any case been discredited by the failure in Lisbon. English soldiers would serve in Brittany and Normandy, as well as continuing their commitments to their Dutch allies in the Low Countries. And most of the English fleet would remain on watch in the Channel or engage in short cruises to ascertain what the Spanish fleet was up to. The initiative at sea, at least in home waters, thus passed to the Spaniards, much to the dismay of naval historians who feel that the defeat of the Spanish Armada should have led to greater things. However, such a policy with its moderate cost made perfect sense to Elizabeth and her councillors whose main aim was simply to contain and wear down Spain as cheaply as possible and who had no desire to anticipate the world of Nelson.

Such a defensive policy did not mean that the aggressive plundering instincts of England's seamen would have no field in which to operate. In 1587, Sir John Hawkins, the treasurer of the navy, had written a paper called 'A discourse for obtaining a good peace' in which he had described a naval policy which seemed eminently suitable in the new circumstances. 'In the continuance of this war,' he wrote, 'I wish it to be ordered in this sort, that first we have as little to do in foreign countries as may be (but of mere necessity), for that breedeth great charge and no profit at all.'

Instead, he advocated a policy of blockade which would cut Spain off from the vital imports of treasure which she drew every year from her silver-rich colonies in America. The seas between Spain and the Azores should be held continuously by a squadron of six of the Queen's most powerful warships and six smaller auxiliaries. The objective of this fleet would be to capture as much enemy merchant shipping as possible and, in particular, to capture the treasure fleets as they returned from Havana via the Azores to Seville, which 'if we might once strike, our peace were made with honour, safety and profit.' The English fleet would be financed on a joint-stock basis, the Queen's involvement being confined to the cost of equipping the royal ships for which she would receive the shipowner's customary one-third of all prize money. Hawkins thought that it would 'be a very bad and unlucky month' in which such a fleet did not bring in three times its running cost, 'for they can see nothing but it will hardly escape them'.

Experience had shown that four months was as long as a fleet could remain effective at sea, after which time the ships would become too foul and weather-battered to maintain efficiency, water and victuals would have been consumed, and the men would be dying in droves from the inevitable shipboard diseases. Hawkins therefore planned for his squadrons to be replaced every four months by a fresh squadron from England, thus leaving at any one time one squadron of six powerful ships at sea in the Atlantic, one in port refitting and two other squadrons of six ships each permanently in home waters to defend the Channel.[5]

Something very similar to Hawkins's policy was to be adopted for the next few years of the war. England never had the will or the organization to hold the seas between Spain and the Azores continuously with successive squadrons as Hawkins had envisaged. Invasion scares, delays in fitting out ships, divisions and disagreements at home all prevented anything like a continuous blockade being achieved, a task which would have stretched the resources of Nelson's navy 200 years later. As a result, there were often gaps of several months between the dispatch of squadrons, a window of safety through which the Spaniards gratefully shipped much-needed treasure and tropical goods back to Spain. Hawkins's policy was also modified or augmented by the sending of a second squadron to lie off the coast of Spain, as a long stop if the Azores fleet should miss the treasure fleet and as a means of keeping an eye on any sign of activity by Spanish warships in Lisbon or in the ports of northern Spain, fear of invasion being a continuing preoccupation of the English government. Both squadrons also tended to economize in their use of the Queen's ships by employing large privateers or armed merchantmen in their place. Nevertheless, Hawkins's basic ideas were not eclipsed. The war at sea was to be a war against commerce fought by small numbers of royal ships financed and equipped on a joint-stock basis and supported and extended by huge numbers of privateers operating on the European coast, in the Atlantic and in the West Indies.

The focus now moves to one of these campaigns, that which was planned for the summer of 1591. This once again comprised an inshore squadron and a squadron which was to lie in wait for the treasure fleet in the waters of the Azores, only the third such squadron to set sail since the new policy had first been adopted in the autumn of 1589.[6] This is some indication of the lack of realism in Hawkins's policy of continuous blockade and his calculations of profitability had also been over-optimistic. There had been some successes, but not nearly as many prizes had been taken as expected and nothing that could really be called a treasure ship. The sea area to be covered was too large, the delays between fleets too long and the opportunities of slipping past the English among the islands of the Azores too great for total success. Nevertheless, the squadrons had seriously disrupted the timetables of the fleets from America and thus made the lives of King Philip and Spanish merchants more difficult. Indeed, so great was this impact that the treasure fleets due to return to Spain in the summer of 1590 did not set sail and wintered in Havana. It was therefore a double fleet carrying the treasure and produce of two years that the English set out to intercept in 1591, a tantalizing prospect for those who invested in the campaign.

The English fleet which was to sail to the coast of Spain consisted mainly of privateer ships paid for by and under the command of the Earl of Cumberland, the jousting prince of privateers who flew his flag in the Queen's ship *Garland*, the only royal ship in his squadron. The fleet for the Azores was financed jointly by the Queen, Sir Walter Raleigh and the Lord Admiral Howard of Effingham, these last two and their partners putting up most of the money needed to set out the expedition. The fleet initially consisted of six Queen's ships, together with pinnaces, privateers and a number of merchant ships to act as victuallers. Command was given to the Lord Admiral's kinsman, Lord Thomas Howard, the thirty-year-old son of the Duke of Norfolk whose only previous sea service had been in the defence against the Armada when he had been knighted at sea for 'conspicuous bravery'. Howard flew his flag in the *Defiance*, whose victualling he financed, and the original plan was for Sir Walter Raleigh to serve as vice-admiral in the *Revenge*, considered by most observers to be the finest galleon in the Elizabethan navy. However, in March 1591, a last-minute change of plan led to the replacement of Raleigh as vice-admiral of the fleet and commander of the *Revenge* by his kinsman Sir Richard Grenville.

CHAPTER THREE

A MAN OF QUALITY

Was he devil or man?
He was devil for aught they knew.[1]

'GRENVILLE HIMSELF IS something of a mystery, and his career might
be worth recovering,' wrote the historian James A. Williamson in
1927. 'The blaze of ferocious valour in which he met his end is not con-
sistent with a life spent mainly in adding field to field in peaceful Devon;
yet that is almost all that can at present be said of it.'[2] Within a decade
of Williamson's challenge, two biographies of Grenville appeared which
certainly enhance our knowledge of their subject, though the authors were
unable to ascertain what Grenville was doing during long periods for which
there are no sources.[3] Hence there is still something of a mystery about the
life and career of a man who is one of the most famous of that generation
of dreamers and men of action who enlivened the last half of the reign of
Elizabeth.

Richard Grenville was probably born in June 1542 — the exact date is not
known — and just three years later he was to lose his father, Roger, who was
captain of the ill-fated and now very well-known *Mary Rose*, one of the finest
ships of the navy of Henry VIII which capsized and sank off Portsmouth in
1545 with the loss of nearly everyone aboard. In 1550, Richard's grandfather
and namesake, Sir Richard Grenville, a former marshal of the still English
port of Calais, also died and so left the young boy as head of the great
west-country family of Grenville, a family who 'from the Conquest to the
Restoration . . . constantly resided amongst their country men, except when
the public service called upon them to sacrifice their lives for it'.[4]

Nothing is known of Richard Grenville's education, but it was no
doubt 'in every respect suitable to his family and fortune, both being
as fair as any gentleman could boast in the west of England'.[5] He could

read and write and express himself forcefully, if not with the eloquence of some of his contemporaries, and had presumably acquired the typical education of an Elizabethan country gentleman, either from tutors at home or in some west-country grammar school. Such an education would have provided him with at least a smattering of Latin, a Christian faith, a sense of public duty and an admiration for the civilization of the Romans whose ideals of service, courage and stoical acceptance of fate the young Richard certainly seems to have absorbed. One must also assume that he received the military education of his class and that, by the age of seventeen, when he was admitted as a student at the Inner Temple, he could handle arms and strike a fine pose on a horse.

The Inner Temple, like the other Inns of Court, offered young gentlemen a modicum of legal knowledge which might become useful when they came into their estates and also introduced them to the pleasures of the great city of London. One such pleasure was fighting and it was in a street off the Strand that in 1562 Richard Grenville was to kill his first man when, in an upper-class brawl, he ran his sword through a gentleman of London, 'giving him a mortal wound, six inches in depth and one and a half in breadth', an offence for which he was subsequently pardoned.[6] Such upper-class violence was not uncommon in an age when all men of birth were bursting with pride and self-importance and all wore swords, but this insight into the otherwise unknown career of the young Richard Grenville would seem to be in character, for he was certainly a man of violence in middle age.

A brief interval of domesticity, in which he came into his very considerable estates and got married, was followed by his introduction to fighting on a grander scale. The venue for this was the Great Hungarian Plain where Grenville went in 1566 to fight the Turks. Following the wars was the Elizabethan equivalent of the Grand Tour, though it was unusual to travel quite so far to fight and it must have been an exciting experience for Grenville and the band of young west-country bloods who accompanied him. What Grenville did in Hungary is not known, but it seems probable that it was this experience alone which gave him his later reputation as a martial man, for the legend that he fought alongside the Spaniards at the battle of Lepanto in 1571 is almost certainly apocryphal. The only other military experience which he had as a young man was in Ireland where he spent part of 1568 and 1569, earning some distinction as Sheriff of Cork in a difficult situation but winning no spurs on the battlefield.

Grenville, in fact, was no great captain in the sixteenth-century military tradition, nor did he follow the Elizabethan pattern of earning a reputation at court or even at sea, at least not before 1585 when he was in his early forties. Instead Grenville made his name as a great country gentleman who did his duty in his county with businesslike distinction. This meant a life spent among an extensive west-country cousinage, in hunting, visits and 'in adding field to field', but it also meant demanding service as Member of Parliament, deputy lieutenant, justice of the peace and, in 1577, as Sheriff of Cornwall. The highlight of his year as sheriff was the capture and bringing to trial of a Catholic priest who was hung, drawn and quartered and the setting in motion of a drive against papists which virtually extinguished Catholicism in the West Country. This was no more than his duty, as the laws against papists were there to be enforced, but it was more than many other sheriffs were prepared to do and Grenville did his duty with true Protestant gusto. He himself led the well-armed party which brought the priest to justice and he confronted the owner of the house where the priest was concealed with 'his hand upon his dagger as though he would have stabbed it into the gentleman'.[7] Ironically, it was for this aggressive service against papists and not for some great blaze of valour at sea or on the battlefield that one of the most famous fighters in English history was knighted.

Sir Richard's public service in the West Country was paralleled by a growing interest in affairs of the sea, though as yet this interest seems to have been carried out by proxy. The lives of the landed gentry of Devon and Cornwall were often interwoven with matters maritime and Sir Richard was no different from his contemporaries in this respect. He played a major role, for instance, in the transformation of the sleepy fishing port of Bideford, of which the Grenvilles were overlords, into one of the most thriving ports of the West Country. He saw it as no derogation of his birth to engage in trade nor to be a shipowner and was to own several trading ships in the course of his life. Trading in Elizabethan England often developed into

privateering and piracy, especially in the West Country, and in the early
1570s Grenville was part-owner of a small fleet of private men-of-war, one
of which, the *Castle of Comfort*, a well-gunned ship of 240 tons, was to earn
considerable notoriety under a commission from the French Huguenots 'to
pass unto the seas in warlike sort to apprehend and take all the enemies
of God, called papists'.[8] Grenville seems to have sold the *Castle of Comfort*
by 1575, but he was to have shares in many other private men-of-war as
did his famous Devonian contemporaries such as Drake, Hawkins and Sir
Walter Raleigh. However, there is no evidence that Grenville ever sailed or
fought on such ships. The description of him by a Spanish agent in 1574
as *'gran corsario'*, great corsair or pirate, is almost certainly prophetic rather
than accurate and may well reflect an understandable Spanish view that all
west-country gentlemen were at least tainted with piracy.[9]

The remark was made in relation to a project which Grenville and
some partners had proposed to the Queen early in 1574, a project which
demonstrates that, if he had not yet any reputation as a man of the sea, he
would certainly have liked to gain one. Grenville's great enterprise was 'for
discovery of sundry rich and unknown lands', a voyage to the South Pacific
through the Straits of Magellan. This would incorporate the settling of an
English colony in the southern tip of South America or perhaps in the as
yet undiscovered continent thought to lie in the South Pacific, an area
which had been 'by God's providence reserved for England'.[10] Interest in
the geography of the Pacific had been stimulated in recent years by the
news of the Spanish conquest of the Philippines in 1564, their pioneering of
a safe (or fairly safe) route back across the Pacific in the following year and
by Mendaña's discovery in 1567 of the Solomon Islands which he took to be
the fringe of the great southern continent. Grenville's proposal was couched
in a spirit of geographical enquiry and benign imperialism, but there seems
little doubt from the force of the ships which he proposed to take with him
that plunder was not far from the front of his mind. But it was not to be.
The Queen had no wish to upset the Spaniards, with whom at this time
she was on amicable terms, and she rejected the petition. Grenville never
sailed to the South Pacific and both the glory and the plunder were to fall
just three years later to another man of Devon, Sir Francis Drake, who set

off on very much the same route to circumnavigate the globe in 1577 and 1578.

Grenville retained an interest in imperialism, plunder, glory and the sea, but it was public business in Cornwall and Devon that was to occupy him for the decade following the rejection of his great project. His chance was to come in 1585 when, at the last moment, Sir Walter Raleigh was forbidden by the Queen to go on his planned voyage to colonize Virginia and Grenville accepted an invitation to take the command in his place, for the 'love he bare unto Sir Walter Raleigh, togither with a disposition he had to attempt honorable actions worthie of honour'.[11] It is somewhat ironic that both of the adventurous commands which were to make Grenville famous in English history, in 1585 and 1591, were only given to him as a substitute for the more famous Sir Walter Raleigh. But so it was, and Grenville was not a man to let slip such opportunities for fame and glory.

It was only with his two voyages to Virginia in 1585 and 1586 that Sir Richard Grenville became a great man of the sea and so acquired the beginnings of the reputation that he has maintained to this day. Indeed, it seems probable that it was not until the age of forty-two that he actually went to sea — that is with the exception of such short voyages as were necessary to get to Ireland or Hungary. It was with these Virginia voyages too that he began to be very well known to the Spaniards and so to acquire his almost diabolical reputation as a *gran corsario*, a description which, as we have seen, was only prophetic in 1574.

The proposal to establish a colony in Virginia was ostensibly a peaceful one which merely aimed to create a self-sufficient settlement in lands as yet untouched by Europeans, but in fact it was far from peaceful and was very much an act of war. In the first place, it was a challenge to the Spaniards who laid claim to this territory and who, twenty years previously, had destroyed a French Huguenot colony in Florida. More importantly, this first English colony in America, at Roanoke Island in what is now North Carolina, was designed principally as a base from which to attack the Spanish treasure fleets whose passage home ran up the coast of Florida and then east or north-east towards Bermuda. It seems probable too that Grenville's voyage in 1585 was planned in conjunction with Drake's great raid to the West Indies in

PLATE 1 *Detail of Thomas Hood's chart of the North-*
east Atlantic, 1592.

A^N · DÑI · 1571 ·
ÆTATIS · SVÆ
· 29 ·

Sir Richard Granville, killed
in a sea-fight near the Azores,
1591

PLATE 2 *Sir Richard Grenville, aged 29, by an unknown artist.*

PLATE 3 *An English galleon, probably the* Revenge, *in action during the battle of the Armada, by Hendrick C. Vroom.*

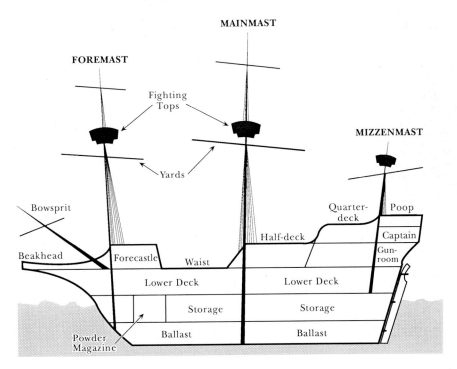

DIAGRAM 1 *Sketch plan of an Elizabethan galleon.*

PLATE 4 *Map of the siege of Smerwick Bay, 1580,
showing English ships including the* Revenge.

the same year — two aspects of the same policy which made inevitable the long war between England and Spain.

The colonizing experiment at Roanoke was a failure and it was not to be until the next century that England built up her great empire in America. The disappointment of failure was however mitigated by the fact that these voyages to America made a profit for their backers. This was due to Sir Richard Grenville's great successes as a privateer, perhaps we should say corsair, in these his first excursions into the maritime world of plunder. On his first outward voyage, he took two Spanish frigates off Puerto Rico, one 'with good and rich freight', which were ransomed for a good sum. And, soon after he left America to return to England, he took a ship rich enough to cover the costs of the whole voyage, 'a tall ship of four hundred tons or thereabouts, making the same course that he did, unto whom he gave chase, and in a few hours by goodness of sail overtook, and by violence won, richly laden with sugar, hides, spices and some quantity of gold, silver and pearl: she was the vice-admiral of Sancto Domingo that year for Spain.'[12] Grenville transferred his flag to the prize and, on his way home, called at the island of Flores in the Azores, an island which later was to get to know him very well, though on this occasion he simply forced the islanders to give him some much-needed provisions.

Grenville returned to Virginia in the following year to take supplies to the colonists whom he had left behind under the command of Ralph Lane, only to find that the colony had already been abandoned and the men shipped home with the fleet of Drake on his return from his ravages in the West Indies. Any anger or frustration that Grenville might have felt at this disappointment was taken out on the people of the Azores, his second visit to the islands being rather longer than his first. His activities are succinctly described by Richard Hakluyt, the contemporary propagandist of English naval expansion. Grenville, he reports, 'fell with the Isles of Acores, on some of which Ilandes he landed, and spoyled the townes of all such thinges as were worth carriage, where also he took divers Spanyardes'.[13] No wonder his reputation should have preceded him when he returned to the islands five years later, in the summer of 1591.

Grenville's first appearance on a world stage in 1585 and 1586 provides an opportunity to see him as others saw him as he made his entrée into history. Here was certainly a competent commander, able to do what he set out to do, to lead other men by fear or example, to quell disputes and to make difficult decisions when they had to be made. Here, too, was a great English gentleman whose style enormously impressed visitors or prisoners who came into his ship. 'This Richard Grenville appeared to be a man of quality,' wrote a merchant of Lisbon who was a passenger on one of Grenville's prizes. 'He was served with much show, and vessels of silver and gold, and servants, and many musical instruments which they played while he ate.'[14] A fine gentleman he was, to dine at sea to the music of trumpets and clarions, but Sir Richard also had many of the faults of his class. In particular, he was an extremely domineering and proud man, 'the most arrogant man in the world' as a Spaniard described him, while Ralph Lane complained of his 'intolerable pride and unsaciable ambition'.[15]

One finds too a somewhat crazy sense of adventure in this fine English gentleman, if we can believe Hakluyt who described Grenville's capture of the rich prize from Santo Domingo. Having no suitable boat to board the prize, he is said to have fabricated a raft from some empty chests, a fragile vessel 'which fell a sunder and sunke at the shippe's side', as Grenville swarmed on to the Spanish ship at the head of his men. One wonders if it was normal practice for the commander of a ship to lead such a boarding party in person. One wonders too if it was customary for the captain to conduct in person the search for valuable goods on a captured ship as Grenville did.[16]

There is a savagery too and a wanton love of destruction in many of his actions. On his way out to Virginia, he called at Puerto Rico to collect water and provisions and, on his departure, burned the fort which he had built to defend himself and for good measure fired the woods as well. In Virginia, we find him once again busy with the torch as he fires an Indian village in reprisal for the theft of a silver cup, one among several harsh actions which turned the Indians, 'the most gentle, loving and faithful' people, into men filled with hatred who would destroy the infant colony.

In the Azores too, he was ready to burn and destroy to satisfy his hatred of papists, so that it is small wonder that he 'was greatlie feared in these

islands and known of every man', as we learn from the Dutch merchant
Linschoten who was resident in the islands. The same author provides an
illuminating picture of Grenville dining with some Spanish captains in the
Azores. 'He would carouse three or foure glasses of wine, and in a braverie
take the glasses betweene his teeth and crash them in peeces and swallow
them downe, so that often times the blood ran out of his mouth without
any harme at all unto him.' True or not, such a story could only be told
of a man of 'hard complection', as Linschoten described him.[17]

It is then a domineering, proud, violent man with an insatiable hatred
of Spaniards and papists who is the hero of this book, a gentleman but a
dangerous and not very nice one. Something of this may be glimpsed in
the portrait by an unknown artist in the National Portrait Gallery. Grenville
was twenty-nine when this was painted and he was a handsome man. But the
watchful eyes, the cruel line of the mouth and the set of the shoulders suggest
the anger behind the elegance. One is not too surprised that this young man
should grow into the rapacious corsair whose deeds and personality became
so notorious throughout the Spanish Empire.

This notoriety was possibly assisted by the ease with which his name
could be hispanicized. Most Englishmen appear in Spanish documents in
some terribly mutilated version of their name, but not Grenville whose
surname in the later sixteenth century was normally spelt and pronounced
as Greenfield, a word which is easy to translate into Castilian. And so Sir
Richard becomes Don Ricardo de Campoverde, which has a fine flourish
and somehow suits the personality of the man. It is so much easier to hate
someone whose name you can pronounce.

Spain was used to English corsairs, but there are few who so quickly
gripped the Spanish imagination with a mixture of admiration and fear
as did Don Ricardo de Campoverde. Spaniards admired his qualities as
a gentleman, his *arrogancia*, that almost insane pride which determined the
behaviour of the Spanish *hidalgo*. They feared the man who was '*gran marinero
y corsario y mayor hereje y perseguidor de catolicos*', a great sailor and corsair, and
great heretic and persecutor of Catholics.

How different this assessment is from that accorded to Lord Thomas
Howard who was to command Grenville in the campaign of 1591, '*hombre*

moço y no marinero', a mere youngster and no sailor. Howard was indeed a very different sort of man from Grenville, 'that most noble Lord Howard whose exceeding great magnanimity, courage, and wisdome, joyned with such an honourable kind of sweet courtesy, bounty and liberality as . . . hath wonne him all the faithfull loving hearts of as many as ever have had any manner of dealing with him'. It would be unthinkable that anyone should write such words of Grenville, whose 'owne people hated him for his fierceness and spake very hardly of him'.[18]

This then was the man who returned from his second voyage to America late in 1586 to find an England busy making itself ready to face the threat of Spanish invasion. Grenville was to be as busy as anyone in the next few years, but his life would lack the glamour and glory of many of his maritime contemporaries, partly because it was believed that he was not a man who would obey orders without question. In June 1587, an English squadron was to be sent to reinforce Drake after the famous raid on Cadiz in which he 'singed the King of Spain's beard'. 'It was proposed in the council,' reported a Spaniard, 'that Grenville, a gentleman who has always sailed with pirates, should command the squadron, but it was objected that he would not serve under Drake and it was necessary to send some other person who would not raise questions but would obey Drake unreservedly.'[19] Grenville's biographers explain this comment in terms of Grenville's jealousy of Drake, a social inferior who had outshone him in the eyes of the world and who had stolen his thunder in the 1570s with his encircling of the globe. This may be true, but it seems just as probable that this is another example of Grenville's *arrogancia* and that it was felt likely that he would disobey any order with which he disagreed, whether given by Drake or anyone else.

Grenville's failure to get this command in 1587 did not prevent his role in the defence against the Armada from being an important one. His task was to co-ordinate the defences of Cornwall and Devon which seemed one of the most likely places for a Spanish landing. Forts and castles were repaired under his supervision and trained bands were drilled, while he sent several of his own ships to reinforce the English fleet at Plymouth. But Grenville himself remained on land as commander of the west for most of the Armada campaign, only going to sea to watch for Spanish ships still capable of a threat when they came south after rounding Scotland. Later, he went to Ireland and remained there until late in 1590, at first engaged in rounding up Spanish survivors from the Armada and then playing an active part in the repeopling of Munster with English settlers after the devastation of the province in the great Desmond rebellion.

Grenville acquired more land than any of the other undertakers of this English colonization of south and south-west Ireland and his approach to the difficult task of settlement showed the same businesslike qualities which he was always able to direct to affairs of the land. Still, though potentially very profitable, this must have been dull work compared with commanding a ship and one can imagine his delight when he received a letter from the Queen summoning him to court 'for some courses of service'. This service turned out to be command of the *Revenge*, a fine ship in which to show the Queen and the world what a great captain he could be.

CHAPTER FOUR

THE FINEST GALLEON IN THE WORLD

For strength, assurance, nimbleness
and swiftness of sailing, there are . . .
no vessels to be compared with ours.[1]

'MY LORD THOMAS HOWARD hath kissed her Majesty's hand, and is gone down to his ships, Sir Richard Grenville being his Vice-admiral, and they and their partners I assure your Lordship make a very goodly fleet. God send them good speed, and a safe return.'[2] The date was 10 March, high time for the 1591 campaigning season to be getting under way and time for us to take a look at the *Revenge*.

Few ships in the history of naval warfare have been so praised by contemporaries, praise which is echoed by naval historians. Sir Geoffrey Callender described her as 'the strongest and lordliest weapon of sea-warfare afloat'; Sir Julian Corbett said she was 'considered by Drake a masterpiece of naval construction and his ideal of what a great-ship should be'. The Spaniards were just as enthusiastic in their praise. The *Revenge* was 'the best that they have in England', '*uno de los mas lindos galeones del mundo*', one of the finest galleons in the world.[3] What sort of ship could earn such epithets?

The *Revenge* had been built in 1577 by Matthew Baker of Deptford, most famous of Elizabethan shipwrights. Since then, she had given sterling service to Queen and country, in Ireland and the West Indies, the Channel and the Azores and, most notably, as Drake's flagship in the defence against the Armada when the *Revenge* had been in the thick of the gun fight off the banks of Flanders and had been 'pierced with shot above forty times, and his very cabben was twice shot through'.[4] She was the epitome of the new 'race-built' galleons which were the pride of the Elizabethan navy, so much so that orders for new galleons very often simply specified that they should be built on the model of the *Revenge*. These new galleons were built for speed, strength and nimbleness, as has been seen, with sleek lines ensured by a high keel-to-beam ratio and with a fairly drastic reduction in the superstructure of castles fore and aft which had been such a feature of the great fighting ships of the past. They were not very big, medium-size by the standards of the day and small by those of later periods, smaller than the smallest frigate in Nelson's navy. The *Revenge* herself was 92 feet at the keel and, with her rake forward and aft, perhaps 130 to 140 feet overall. She measured just 441 tons, though normally rated at 500, a graceful but very solid fighting machine whose double line of gunports looked very dangerous as she sat low and sturdy in the water.

There is only one well-authenticated picture of the *Revenge* which was drawn in 1580 to commemorate a battle fought in Smerwick Bay in Ireland. The *Revenge* was the flagship on this occasion and the artist drew sketches of all the ships involved and seems to have taken care to be accurate. It can be seen that the *Revenge* had a very low forecastle, barely breaking the line of the upper deck aft of the foremast, but that she had a much higher superstructure in her stern than some descriptions of race-built galleons would lead one to expect. These after-works started aft of the mainmast and rose in two steps to the half-deck and then to the quarter-deck or poop where there was a large stern-lantern. The forecastle and after-works had very solid bulwarks facing the waist of the ship to provide defence against boarders, while aft there was an impressively high and narrow stern built out over the sea, a fine feature of the Elizabethan galleon which incorporated much intricate carving, but did not yet match up to the magnificent baroque sterns of a century later. The after-works contained the captain's cabin, no doubt with the fine gold and silver plate which Grenville had carried on previous voyages, and also housed the cabins of the more senior mariners, the steerage, the gun-room and lower down such storage compartments as the bread-room. All the upper-works of the *Revenge* were painted in a handsome pattern of green and white squares and diagonals.

The bows of the *Revenge* are obscured by gunsmoke in this picture, but, like all galleons of the period, she would have had a great ornate beakhead built out over the water to provide a platform for sailors to work the sails on the foremast and on the bowsprit which stuck out in front of the ship at an angle of about thirty degrees. The beakhead also functioned as a heads or latrine, though many disdained such an arrangement and used the bilge instead, leaving a stench so powerful that it could cause men to pass out and plunge to a horrible death.

Many galleons of the late sixteenth century had four masts, but the *Revenge* had only three, each fitted with large round 'tops' for look-outs and as a fighting platform from which men could fire into an enemy ship. The main- and foremasts, each with a topmast, but probably not a topgallant mast, carried four large square sails altogether. These were often finely decorated and were still cut fairly full by later standards. Topmasts could be lowered by this date, quite a recent innovation, as of course could the wooden yards which lay across the masts and carried the sails. In addition to her two principal masts, the *Revenge* had a mizzen which rose from the poop and carried lateen main and topsails, while a large rectangular spritsail was hung from the bowsprit. Artists rarely drew rigging in detail, but one has to imagine several hundreds of yards of spiders' webs of rope and cable, great lattice-works of shrouds and stays to support the masts and to provide access to the yards and tops, and a maze of halyards and lifts, parrels and braces, bowlines and clewlines, sheets and tacks to enable the sailors to manoeuvre the yards and sails. And capping all was a profusion of flags and decorative banners and streamers, often twenty or thirty feet long, which fluttered in the breeze as it filled the great windbag sails.

About half-way between the forecastle bulkhead and the mainmast, the main hatchway gave access to the lower deck. There were also smaller hatchways or scuttles leading down below from the forecastle itself and from the quarter-deck, while gratings gave further ventilation for the lower deck and provided an outlet for the smoke of the guns and the general and all-pervading stink of humanity, filth and bilge. Hatchways were fitted with coamings to keep out the sea and these were pierced with loopholes to provide further firing stations should the ship be boarded, the angle of fire ensuring a particularly unpleasant wound as the boarders were 'shot in between the legges, the bullets issuing forth at their breasts'.[5]

It was on the lower deck that the great guns of the galleon were mounted, each with its rectangular gunport fitted with a hinged lid to keep the sea out in rough weather or when the ship heeled, the bottom of the ports being about four feet above water level in calm weather. It was also on the lower deck, an area only some thirty feet wide and five or six feet high, that the ship's company was berthed, although the arrangements for this are somewhat obscure in descriptions of galleons. Hammocks were not introduced until 1597 and the men bedded down on the deck itself, their bedding being rolled up like sandbags to provide protection in a fight. What is not clear is whether the lower deck was simply a large open space or whether it was divided into compartments or cabins. Some accounts suggest an open space cluttered up with the beds, chests and trunks of the crew, a clutter which discommoded the gunners as they worked the cannon in a fight. Others suggest that there were at least some cabins between decks whose walls were quickly taken down to clear the ship for action. Sir Walter Raleigh, for instance, referred to deck cabins, but did not approve of them. 'They are but sluttish dens that breed sickness, serving to cover stealths, and in fight are dangerous to tear men with their splinters.'[6]

Below the lower deck was the hold of the galleon which certainly was divided into several parts by bulkheads to provide such storage as the powder magazine forward, the cable tier, carpenter's and boatswain's stores and storage for beer and provisions aft. Where the galley was on an Elizabethan galleon is not quite clear. Some writers have it right down on the gravel ballast at the bottom of the ship, this being considered the only really safe place to have a fire — that greatest scourge of the wooden ship. Others place the galley on the false orlop deck, a short deck amidships below the lower deck but above the ballast. And some have it in the forecastle, though this is seen as rather too close to the powder magazine for comfort.

Wherever it was, the galley would have been set on brickwork for safety and its equipment seems to have been minimal — little more than some huge kettles in which to boil everything and a few ladles. This was all that was necessary for the provisions issued to the sailors which, though substantial, were hardly designed for variety of diet. There is a record of two months' stores sent out to the 1,140 men in the six royal ships of Lord Thomas Howard's fleet. These consisted of 265 barrels of beer, enough for a weekly ration of six gallons per head, 28 tons of ship's biscuit, 8 tons of bacon, 285 quarters of peas, 2,800 pounds of salt butter, 5,700 pounds of cheese and 5,700 pieces of the dried salt cod known as stock-fish. There was no fresh meat, except in home waters, no fresh fruit or vegetables, though these were already known to combat scurvy, and if there were any concessions to the delights of the kitchen at all they must have been included in the item called 'necessaries at fourpence the man'.[7] Such food quickly became rotten and the beer flat and sour, major factors in the diseases which regularly decimated the crews of all ships, but perhaps especially those of the Queen. The sailor's life was thus extremely unpleasant — constantly wet and tired in smelly, cramped surroundings and fed on foul food and flat beer in these days a hundred years before rum became standard navy fare and even longer before hot drinks such as tea or coffee became the common cheering drink of seafaring men.

The *Revenge* then was handsome to the outside eye, but squalid within, though by most accounts not quite as squalid as the galleons of Spain which were even more crowded with humanity who had to fight for their space with hordes of rats, mice, lice, fleas and bedbugs. For all that, the *Revenge* was as efficient a fighting machine as the age could produce. This was mainly because of her guns which, even more than her strength and sleek lines, were what attracted contemporary admiration, 'the finest artillery which has ever been seen in a sailing ship' as a Spaniard put it.[8] Conflicting data exist for the guns of the *Revenge* but it seems probable that on her last voyage she carried forty-two guns, all made of bronze, most of them mounted on the efficient truck carriages which were not yet used on Spanish ships. It is impossible to say exactly what this armament consisted of, the nomenclature and description of guns always being tricky in this period and made more difficult if one consults both English and Spanish descriptions. However, the broad picture is fairly clear.[9]

The most striking feature of the guns of the *Revenge* was the size and weight of the twenty cannon on her lower deck, a heavier armament than was carried on Spanish galleons several hundred tons larger. These were the ship-battering guns which have been seen by naval historians as the essence of English naval tactics during this period. The biggest were the two demi-cannon, the heaviest cannon carried on ships of the time which shot iron cannon-balls weighing between 20 and 30 pounds. Only slightly smaller were the four cannon-perriers which threw stone or iron shot weighing 20 to 24 pounds. These six heavy cannon would probably have been mounted amidships. So far, the *Revenge* was not particularly unusual for a powerful ship of the day. What was really striking was that, in addition, her lower-deck battery carried no less than ten culverins, long-barrelled cannon firing iron shot of about 17 or 18 pounds, the remaining four guns on the lower deck being demi-culverins with shot weighing 8 or 9 pounds. This balance made the armament of the *Revenge* very powerful indeed, for the ratio between the numbers of culverins and demi-culverins was normally the other way round. All these cannon were muzzle-loading and they were probably arranged in two broadsides of eight cannon each side, with two guns firing out of the stern and two of the long culverins as bow-chasers.

The *Revenge*'s upper-deck battery was as usual much lighter but was still formidable, comprising four more demi-culverins, eight to ten sakers, small muzzle-loading cannon firing shot of 4 or 5 pounds, and an assortment of small breech-loading guns such as perriers, falcons and fowlers. The latter were mainly anti-personnel weapons and were often mounted on swivels on the deck-coaming or in the forecastle and half-deck bulkheads for firing into the waist of the ship to repel boarders. The total weight of this fearsome collection of ordnance was quite staggering for a ship of the size of the *Revenge*. We have seen earlier that English ships were heavily gunned compared with Spanish ships, with a ratio of weight of guns to tonnage of some 8 to 10 per cent as opposed to 3 to 4 per cent. A recent estimate suggests that the ratio for the *Revenge* was as much as 14 per cent of her tonnage, though this is probably too high as it is based on a Spanish assessment of the weight of her guns which is almost certainly an exaggeration.[10] Nevertheless, there is no doubt that the *Revenge* and other English ships like her were the most heavily gunned ships of their size in the late sixteenth-century world.

One ship which must have been very like the *Revenge* was the *Defiance*, Lord Thomas Howard's flagship which had been built on the model of the *Revenge* in 1588 and like her was rated at 500 tons and was supposed to carry 250 men. The *Nonpareil* which was commanded by Sir Edward

Denny and was to join the other five Queen's ships in late March was also the same size. The *Bonaventure* which had been Drake's flagship in 1585 and 1587 and was now commanded by his old captain, Robert Crosse, was the biggest galleon in Lord Thomas's fleet at 600 tons, while the *Crane*, a ship recently built on Dutch lines, was 200 tons and the *Moon*, the midget among the Queen's ships, still had forty men packed into her 60 tons. They must indeed have looked a goodly fleet as Lord Thomas and Sir Richard came down to board them after kissing the Queen's hand in the second week of March 1591.

Much had already been done before that, of course. Fitting-out for a voyage lasting at least four months and probably longer was not something that could be done in a day or two and the *Revenge*'s wages bill started on 4 February when a skeleton crew of forty shipkeepers was taken on to rig the ship. It was in February too that the ship's armament was completed with the delivery of small arms and gunpowder from the Tower armoury. A total of fourteen lasts or 336 barrels containing 100 pounds of gunpowder each were delivered for the five royal ships then in commission, together with 400 muskets and 250 calivers, a light kind of arquebus. The *Revenge*'s share of these, assuming that she received supplies proportional to her tonnage, would have been just over 90 barrels of gunpowder, 110 muskets and about 70 calivers, more firepower to add to the great guns.[11] Nor was this all, for it is clear from inventories of other English ships of the day that bows and arrows still played a role in the lesser armament of galleons, 40 or 50 bows and 80 to 100 sheaves of arrows being usual for the larger ships, as well as large numbers of pikes, bills and swords for hand-to-hand fighting, grenades and other 'fireworks' to which the English attached great importance in a close fight, and morions (helmets) and corselets for protection of the crew's heads and upper bodies. An Elizabethan galleon had to be prepared for everything.

A handsome ship and a formidable armament were not much use without a crew to sail and fight, though the evidence does not exist to say very much about the men who served alongside Sir Richard Grenville on the last voyage of the *Revenge*. We can assume that most of them were young since, despite a few grizzled veterans of the sea, the great majority of Elizabethan seamen were in their twenties. Most writers also assume that the majority of the crew of the *Revenge* came from the ports of Devon, Tennyson for instance suggesting that they were all 'men of Bideford', Grenville's home town.[12] Such assumptions are based on Grenville's fame as a man of the west, on the fact that the *Revenge* finally sailed from Plymouth and on western chauvinism, which assumes that all fighting men of the sea came from Devon and Cornwall and that such men would have knocked each other down in the rush to serve under so famous a captain.

The truth as usual is rather less romantic. The majority of the crew were almost certainly Londoners or east-coast sailors, since the *Revenge* made up the bulk of her numbers before she left the Thames. This is clear from the accounts of Sir Walter Raleigh who paid for the victuals and the wages of the ship. These show that the forty shipkeepers who were rigging the ship in early February had been increased to 100 men by the end of the month and to 160 by 9 March. The *Revenge* sailed from London a week or two later for Portsmouth and Plymouth where she made up her full complement of 260 men.[13]

It also seems unlikely that many of the men were willing volunteers, though possibly the fame of Sir Richard and the nature of the voyage made it slightly less difficult to fill the ship's complement than was sometimes the case on royal ships. This was after all a voyage of plunder and, although the men were paid wages and were not on shares as in a privateering ship, there were well-defined rights of spoil from a captured ship for all members of the crew. Even so, the recruiters clearly had problems as can be seen from an item in Raleigh's accounts. 'To 45 men that fledd from the *Revenge* . . . by ye Lord Admirall's direction to have one shilling and sixpence apeice to returne to the shippe againe,' an amusing reflection on the manning of the Elizabethan navy which seems a world away from the reported horrors of the press-gang in Nelson's day. The men of Devon were no keener to volunteer than their cockney colleagues. When the Privy Council tried to raise men from the port towns of the west in June, their spokesmen pleaded that they were unable to help since there were very few mariners left. Most of them had gone to sea with the privateering ships or fishing to the Newfoundland Banks, while many 'were pressed here hence by the Earl of Cumberland, Lord Thomas

Howard and Sir Richard Grenville at their last being at Plymouth'.[14]

The crew of the *Revenge* was therefore a crew consisting largely of pressed and unwilling men who would much rather have been doing something other than sailing to glory in the Azores. No doubt they dragged their feet until the last moment, as did the men of the *Dainty* before Sir Richard Hawkins's voyage of 1593:

And so I began to gather my company on board, which occupied my good friends and the Justices of the town two days, and forced us to search all lodgings, taverns and alehouses. For some would ever be taking their leave and never depart; some drink themselves so drunk that except they were carried aboard, they of themselves would not be able to go one step.

Once dried out, however, such men were not totally untrained landsmen. Pressed men in the Elizabethan navy were supposed to be sailors and fishermen, men of the sea, but they were generally regarded as the very worst and poorest of their kind who had neither the legs to run away nor the purse to bribe themselves out of the press, the 'tag and rag' who received the scorn of such contemporaries as Sir John Hawkins and Sir Walter Raleigh. 'These poor fishermen and idlers that are commonly presented to his majesty's ships,' wrote Sir Walter a few years later, 'are so ignorant in sea-service, as they know not the name of a rope.'[15]

In contrast to the formal hierarchy in the Spanish navy, there was as yet no system of commissioned officers in the English navy. And so, although one occasionally finds mention of a lieutenant, the captain normally stood supreme as commander of the ship with no one else between him and those senior mariners who today would be called warrant officers. This seems to have been the position on the *Revenge*, the only other commissioned officer apart from Grenville being Captain William Langhorn (or Lahorne), 'as honest man as ever lyveth', who was in command of the soldiers who sailed with the ship.[16] Langhorn's role was an important one, as the only other gentleman in a position of authority, but he was clearly subordinate to Grenville. The captain of a Queen's ship was not usually chosen for his maritime experience, but for his birth, powers of leadership and fighting skills, often acquired on land, and had no need to know anything at all about seamanship and the sea. Grenville was not quite such an innocent in this respect as Lord Thomas Howard, but he is unlikely to have had much practical skill in managing a ship.

This was the job of the senior mariners, men of a different class and well experienced in affairs of the sea, men inured to 'the ordinary hardships of the seaman's lot — a hard cabin, cold and salt meat, broken sleeps, mouldy bread, dead beer, wet clothes, want of fire'.[17] The pay scales for such ships as the *Revenge* show that much the most important mariner was the master, who earned more than twice the wages of anyone else. Next in line was the pilot and then the two mates, the boatswain and the master carpenter, followed by the surgeon, still an artisan rather than an educated gentleman at this date, and the two trumpeters who played the part of heralds on board ship as well as sounding the appropriate calls for every manoeuvre. Given the emphasis on gunnery in all comments on England's ships at this date, it is surprising to find that the master gunner and his two mates were quite lowly paid members of the crew, paid less for instance than the quarter-masters, the coxswain, the purser or even the cook. Altogether, the pay scales allow for thirty-seven men who might be considered as warrant officers and so distinguished from the rest of the sailors, gunners and soldiers who made up the 260 men who set sail in the *Revenge*.[18]

The galleon in fact carried one more man who is very useful to the historian. He was Philip Gawdy, a gentleman adventurer from Norfolk 'without any office in the ship', whose letters home to his elder brother provide some delightful details of the cruise of the *Revenge*. Gawdy was the younger son of a younger son, a gentleman in his late twenties who needed to ingratiate himself with his betters if he was to get on in the world, and he hoped 'to winne much honor' from his adventure. In his first letter relating to the voyage of the *Revenge*, written shortly before she set sail from the Thames, he already appears on good terms with Lord Thomas and Sir Richard whom he was about to accompany to say farewell to the Queen. He, like everyone else, had been rushing around getting his equipment together, 'my apparell will be made to night', while he was proud to tell his brother that he had 'already bought my armes and targett [shield] the very fellowes to my Lord

Thomas and Sir Richard'. This was Gawdy's first sea-voyage and his letter, which is full of profuse goodbyes and commendations, expresses well the mixture of excitement and apprehension of a man about to be 'away as fast as the shippes will fall downe'.[19]

CHAPTER FIVE

INTO THE SUMMER SEA

Serve God daily, love one another,
preserve your victuals,
beware of fire,
and keepe good companie.[1]

Let fall your maine saile, every man say his private prayer for a boone
voyage! Out with your spret saile, on with your bonits and drablers,
steare steady and keep your course, so you go well.

Yachtsmen will recognize the excitement in Captain John Smith's evoca-
tion of that moment when at last the weeks of preparation are over, the
tricky navigation out to sea has been completed and it is time to set sail
after sail to catch the wind of adventure. Some may even remember that
first time when the exotic language of the sea and the strange manoeuvres
and customs of ships were as incomprehensible and vaguely threatening to
them as they no doubt were to Philip Gawdy as he first felt the sails of the
Revenge fill and her bows plunge into the seas. Gawdy was to adapt quickly
and his letters to his brother are soon peppered with the language of the
sailor as he begins to revel in this brave new maritime world. After a few
weeks, he can write that he has now become 'a reasonable good mariner',
proud to 'have travelled farther than any of my name'. There is, however, a
twinge of landsickness in his regret that 'there is not a good alehouse within
twenty leagues of us' and he had become only too aware of the many perils of
the sea: 'It is a place that maketh the most dissolute and dysordered person
lyving to remember God.'[2]

It was not long before Lord Thomas Howard's ships had their first
taste of these dangers as they encountered 'I thinke the extremist furye of
the weather', a March gale in the English Channel. Captain Smith has a

scenario for this as well:

> It over-casts. We shall have wind, fowle weather. Settell your top sailes, take in the spret-saile, in with your top-sailes, lower the fore-saile . . . brade up close all them sailes, lash sure the ordnance, strike your top-masts to the cap.[3]

Taking in sail and making the ship safe sounds easy enough, as Smith describes it, but it must have been a nerve-racking experience in the midst of a gale. What was it like to take in the spritsail when the beakhead was plunging deep into the sea and the bowsprit was bending like a fishing rod? What was it like to take in the topsails or 'brade up close all them sailes' when there were as yet no foot-ropes for sailors to stand on as, high up above the raging sea, they lay straddled with their stomachs on the yards to do their work in the howling gale? They had to cling tight as they took in and lashed the sails, for the hempen ropes supporting the masts gave so much that they threatened to plunge into the sea each time the ship heeled over. The tops and yards of an Elizabethan galleon were no place for landsmen and it is good to find that they were not required to go aloft, their task being to assist the sailors on deck. Not that the decks were particularly comfortable in a storm as the two-ton, lower-deck guns fought against their restraining lashings, the sea poured over the gunwales and the very planks of the ship moved against each other, keeping the crew busy working the endless chain pumps, an invaluable innovation of Elizabethan times, while the carpenter and his mates desperately plugged the leaks which appeared as the timbers of the ship came alive in the wild sea.[4]

Storms were commonplace in the Channel and no doubt novices soon became as blasé as their sailor colleagues when the tempest roared, shrugging off wind, wet, sickness and exhaustion as a necessary part of life at sea. Even so, Philip Gawdy was probably glad when the *Revenge* was safely in Plymouth where he took the opportunity to write another letter to his brother. 'I hope in God it shall not be my last.' The Devon port, like most of the other ports in southern and western England, was bustling with activity as the private men-of-war were prepared for the 1591 hunting season. This business had been attracting more and more investment in recent years and 1591 was probably the peak year in the war so far, with a minimum of 138 separate privateering ships at sea. They were drawn from ports all the way round from Chester to King's Lynn, but the great majority came from London, which sent out nearly fifty ships in this year, and from the ports of south and south-west England. Most privateers operated singly or in small consortships of two or three ships on the seaboard of Europe, from the Baltic to the Mediterranean, wherever there might possibly be prey in the form of the merchant ships of Spain and her allies, such as the Catholic League of France, or of neutrals having goods destined for Spain or Portugal in their holds.[5]

On top of all these little ventures, often in minute ships packed with twenty or thirty men, there were several large-scale expeditions being prepared in the spring of 1591. James Lancaster and George Raymond were fitting out three ships for what turned out to be a disastrous voyage to the East Indies. Thomas Cavendish, who had already blown the huge booty he brought back after circumnavigating the globe in 1588, was preparing to do the trip again — a voyage which was to lead to his death near the island of Ascension. Three separate expeditions, two financed by syndicates of London merchants and the third by Sir George Carey, Captain of the Isle of Wight, were fitting out to sail to the profitable hunting grounds of the West Indies. And then there was that inveterate gambler, the Earl of Cumberland, who was preparing to throw a little more of 'his land into ye sea' as he fitted out the fourth of his eventual total of eleven privateering voyages. This time, it will be remembered, he was to cruise the coast of Spain as a back-up to Lord Thomas Howard in the Azores. His preparations were delayed by money problems and it was not until May that he at last set out with the Queen's ship *Garland* and six of his own ships.[6]

And finally there was Lord Thomas Howard himself whose commission from the Queen permitted him to take any ship he wished into consortship, 'if he should thincke them fitt to serve'. Most of the private men-of-war and victuallers which sailed with him belonged to courtiers and gentlemen who had set out their ships on their own initiative or at the bidding of the Queen and the Lord Admiral who himself owned four of the ships in the fleet.

However, it is clear that Lord Thomas made some use of his commission to swell his fleet while he was in Plymouth, though not without considerable resistance from the men involved, who felt that service in the royal fleet was likely to be irksome and potentially less profitable than the voyages they had planned for themselves. There were in Plymouth, for instance, four powerful ships belonging to the London syndicate headed by the merchant John Watts which were all 'ready furnished and victualed to goe to sea' on their voyage to the West Indies. When Lord Thomas commanded these ships to join his fleet, at least until the end of April, the mariners threatened that 'they would ron awaye' with their ships. The Queen's commission was brandished and the mariners came to heel for the moment, though they were to desert Lord Thomas three weeks later off the coast of Spain and run away to the West Indies, an action which gave rise to the acrimonious lawsuit of Howard v. Watts.[7]

On 5 April 1591, Howard finally set sail from Plymouth with his fleet of royal ships, privateers of all sizes and types from minute pinnaces to galleons, victuallers to carry provisions and the four reluctant ships of John Watts. His instructions have not survived, but the rumours making their way around the West Country would appear to have been accurate. The word was that Howard intended to sail to the coast of Brittany to ensure that there was no Spanish fleet at sea and then via the coast of Portugal to the Azores to await the arrival of the treasure fleets.[8] Reports on the number of ships in his fleet range from ten to forty and such discrepancies reflect reality as well as the inaccuracy of the observers, since the size of the fleet varied almost from day to day. Royal ships returned to port, while others sailed out in their place. Victuallers came and went. Privateers entered into consortship with the Queen's ships for varying lengths of time, while merchant ships sought the protection of the warships for at least part of their voyage. Two undated lists of the ships in Howard's fleet are tabulated below, one drawn up by Lord Thomas himself 'which he sent home from sea' and the other produced by 'the Lord Admiral and others at his Lordship's chamber at Whitehall'. Lord Thomas's list has twenty-three ships and was probably compiled after a month or so at sea, certainly later than 20 April when he lost the services of the ships of John Watts which do not appear in the list.

LORD THOMAS HOWARD'S FLEET

NAME	TONS	MEN	OWNER	1	2
QUEEN'S SHIPS					
Defiance	500	250	The Queen	x	x
Revenge	500	250	The Queen	x	x
Bonaventure	600	250	The Queen	x	x
Nonpareil	500	220	The Queen	x	
Lyon	500	250	The Queen		x
Foresight	360	160	The Queen		x
Crane	200	100	The Queen	x	x
Moon	60	40	The Queen	x	
PRIVATE MEN-OF-WAR AND VICTUALLERS					
Black Lion	200	60	?		x
Chance (Plymouth)	50	30	John Weekes	x	
Charles	80	49	Lord Admiral	x	
Content (Isle of Wight)	?	?	Sir G. Carey	x	
Dainty (Plymouth)	160	95	Sir J. Hawkins	x	
Delight	60	40	Lord Admiral	x	x
Diana (Bridgwater)	60	50	N. Lilbart	x	x
Disdain	70	53	Lord Admiral	x	
Douglass	60	?	?		x
Frances	30	20	Earl of Hertford	x	x
Jonas (Bridgwater)	50	25	W. Denny et al.	x	
Lion (Barnstaple)	?	?	?	x	
Lion (Southampton)	80	50	?	x	
Lyons Whelp	100	50	Lord Admiral	x	x
Mermaid (London)	120	36	W. Bond	x	
Minion (Southampton)	60	40	W. Dudson	x	x
Phoenix (Poole)	80	40	Earl of Hertford	x	x
Pilgrim	120	54	Sir W. Raleigh	x	x
Prudence	100	50	?		x
Galleon Raleigh	250	120	Carew Raleigh	x	x

1. Lord Thomas Howard's list (see text)
2. Lord Admiral's list
Source: BL Lansdowne 70 fos. 171v-172, 229v-230; additional material from Andrews (1964) pp. 243–64.

The Lord Admiral's list of seventeen ships seems to reflect the situation in mid-August, by which date some of the privateers and victuallers had gone home and the original fleet had lost two of the Queen's ships, the *Nonpareil* and the little *Moon* which were sent home in July, and had been reinforced by two others, the 500-ton *Lyon* and the 360-ton *Foresight*.[9]

However many ships there were in Lord Thomas's fleet as they left Plymouth, they were all scattered and driven hither and thither two days later by a gale in the mouth of the Channel which lasted for nearly two weeks. Lord Thomas himself in the *Defiance* and many other ships of the fleet were forced to seek shelter for a day and a night in Falmouth where one of John Watts's privateering ships ran aground. The *Revenge*, as Gawdy tells us in his best maritime language, found herself completely alone and 'tackt about to the wetherward' between the Isles of Scilly and Ushant 'where we did endure very sore weather as might be abiden at the sea'. Both the main and foremasts were 'spent', i.e. broken, by the force of the wind, 'but by Godes grace, they were espyed in good tyme, and strengthened with fishes, wolding and calking, and now thankes be to God, they be in very good plight.'[10] God's help was certainly needed for so hazardous a task as mending a mast in 'very sore weather'.

When the repairs were completed, the *Revenge* continued her voyage southwards across the Bay of Biscay on a very well-worn track for English shipping. Off Cape Finisterre in north-west Spain, they sighted four merchantmen of Hamburg, from whom they took some provisions, and a small flyboat belonging to one of the Catholic League ports of France which was taken as a prize. Sir Richard 'placed a master and [some] of his own men in her, bycause we were alone and had lost all our company'. The *Revenge* and her prize now sailed down the Portuguese coast to the Burlings or Berlingas Islands. This was a favourite place for gathering information from the sardine fishermen of Peniche, who sailed out every night to catch fish off the islands and then sold them in their market to merchants from all over Portugal.

On 18 April, while still near the islands, the masthead look-out saw seven or eight ships, one so big that they thought her 'by her hugeness to be either a Caruke [Portuguese carrack] or an Armada [Spanish man-of-war]'. The *Revenge* cleared for action as she approached the strange ships and then found

that some of them were of our owne fleete, and might easily perceyve that
they had this great ship in chase. There were two pinnaces, the *Lions Whelpp*
and the *Delight*, shott some five or six shott and she never budged. But
presently [immediately] upon our coming in she presently struck her
top sayles and all sayles and yielded herself to Sir Richard Greinfield.

The captured ship which was later declared good prize was the 600-ton
Eagle of Lubeck, a bulky merchant ship valued at £10,000 carrying masts
and planks for the Spanish fleet, a cargo which thus ended up in the English
naval dockyard at Chatham rather than the Spanish one at Corunna. Sir
Richard placed a master and some of his men in the prize, ready to send
her home in a few days, while the *Eagle*'s crew were distributed among the
English ships.[11]

The *Revenge* continued her voyage southwards, past Cascais near Lisbon
where they were so near the shore that 'we might see one of the Kinges
houses', past Cape Espichel and 'so lastly came to the landes end, the
southern cape called Cape St Vincent'. Here, they cruised about for some
time in a vain search for prizes and at last made contact again with Lord
Thomas Howard. 'We hailed my Lord and made great joye to meet him,'
such joy at sea normally being expressed with a salvo of guns, a deafening
fanfare of trumpets and drums and the display of every ensign, flag and
banner that the ships carried. Most of the fleet were now reunited, though
two ships — the Queen's *Moon* and the Lord Admiral's *Disdain* — were still
missing when the fleet set sail for the Azores in the last week of April.

The gales of the Channel became a dim memory as the *Revenge* and the
other ships of Lord Thomas Howard's fleet sailed through 'the southron
seas' due west along the thirty-seventh line of latitude. 'These seas that
we be now in are allmoste as sweet as a ryver in the countrye,' wrote
Philip Gawdy who was revelling in the pleasant sailing conditions and in
his growing self-confidence as a man of the sea. He had 'all ready gotten a
fyne card and other tooles belonging to navigation' and was learning some
of the tricks of the trade from the pilot. Not that navigation was too difficult

as the helmsman steered ever due westward until that moment when the look-outs at the mastheads should espy Santa Maria and São Miguel, the most easterly of the nine islands of the Azores, which lay almost 1,000 miles from the coast of Portugal. Most pilots could manage such a simple course, though it was possible to make a mistake, as did James Hooper, master of the *Desire*, who altered his course against the advice of his shipmates and missed the islands. After beating about for four or five days, he confessed 'that he knewe noe more how the said islands of the Terceiras [i.e. Azores] did bare from him than the maynemast of the shipp did know'.[12]

Nevertheless, most ships made their way westwards to the Azores easily enough and meanwhile Philip Gawdy was finding it all great fun:

I lyke the sea and the sea lyfe and the company at sea, as well as any that ever I lyved withal. The place is good and healthfull to a willing mynde . . . And though there be some stormes endured at sea, yet the end is honorable and sweete and pleasing to any that taketh the course, with which lyfe I am greatly in love allmost as muche as with my Mistress.[13]

Exactly what the routine of that 'lyfe' was is difficult to tell for, although a huge amount has been written about the navy of Queen Elizabeth, both by contemporaries and by historians, this material is usually disappointingly silent on what life was actually like in one of the Queen's ships and much has to be left to the imagination. Even the letters of Philip Gawdy, which are among the most delightful ever written by a newcomer to the sea, provide no enlightenment on the day-to-day routine of a galleon such as the *Revenge*. What information exists comes mainly from manuals and maritime commentaries written by contemporary men of the sea.

Ship's time was kept by the sand glass in the steerage, half an hour to a glass and eight glasses to the watch, the turning of the glass determining such important moments in the sailor's day as dinner at noon and supper at six. The sailors ate in small messes of six or so men, each taking turns to go to the galley to collect the food for their mates. And, since these were Protestant ships engaged in the service of the Lord, divine service was read twice a day before meals, 'or at least (if there be interruption by foul weather) once in the day, praising God every night with a singing of a psalm at the setting of the watch'. This duty was performed at eight in the evening by the trumpeters blowing the appropriate call on their silver instruments. The first watch was the starboard watch under the command of the master:

> Then all the rest may doe what they will till midnight; and then his Mate with his Larboord men, with a Psalme and a Prayer, releeves them till foure in the morning. And so from eight to twelve each other, except some flaw of winde come — some storm or gust — or some accident that requires the helpe of all hands, which commonly, after such good cheere, in most voyages doth happen.[14]

During the day, those not engaged in working the ship were kept busy in the never-ending labour of maintenance and repair — making and mending clothes, swabbing and cleaning, replacing or repairing rigging, sails and yards, loading and unloading muskets and calivers, and drilling on the great guns. Work done, there might be music and dancing to fiddle and drum, as well as ballads and psalms to be sung. Idleness was the root of disorder and good captains took pains to prevent it, Lord Thomas Howard being singled out in this respect in a later voyage: 'So pleasant and curteous [was he] in provoking of them to some one kind of exercise or other, at convenient times to keep them from idleness and sea diseases, a thynge most necessarie.'[15]

In the small moral wooden world of a Protestant galleon, blasphemy was as serious a crime as any maritime lapse and smoking or carrying a naked light below decks was probably the most serious secular sin. Such matters might be treated harshly but, overall, discipline on board was not yet the strict and often savage round of flogging and death one finds in descriptions of the navy during the Napoleonic Wars.[16] Desertion, cowardice, sleeping on watch or even mutiny were often treated with comparative leniency in the Elizabethan navy. Unpleasant punishments were certainly available — ducking from the yard arm, flogging, various forms of mutilation, keel-hauling and so on — but these were not employed very often or if they were we do not hear about it. More frequent were such punishments as being made to swab the ship, a drenching with water, twelve hours in fetters on bread and water or, if it came to a flogging, a touching-up by the boatswain's rod rather than the horrors of the cat.[17] The leadership of captains and senior mariners rather than the existence and enforcement of a savage disciplinary code ensured that crews remained effective fighting units. Such an approach enhanced morale and produced a sense of camaraderie among the crews, despite the high proportion of pressed men in the ships. These men may often have wished that they were somewhere else, but their treatment on board the ships of Lord Thomas Howard's fleet was relatively benign.

Philip Gawdy may have liked the sea and the sea life but he, like everyone else in the fleet, was aware that Lord Thomas Howard's venture had not been very successful as yet, considering the strength and size of the fleet and the large amount of money invested in it. The only worthwhile prize which so many ships had been able to capture in their two weeks or so in the waters of Biscay and off the Portuguese coast had been the great ship from Lubeck which would hardly alone be sufficient to cover much of the investors' outlay. Nothing remotely like a treasure ship had been seen.

Meanwhile, Juan de Texeda, *maestre de campo* or governor of the great Spanish shipping centre of Havana in Cuba, had spent the winter pushing forward the construction of six frigates specially designed for carrying treasure, as fast as almost any vessel afloat and with the strength in armament to fight anything they could not outsail. On 31 January 1591, Texeda was able to report that four of these frigates were now ready to sail for Spain. 'They have cost His Majesty 50,000 ducats and money is still being spent on them. They are built as never were any others which have left this harbour.' On the night of 2 March, when Lord Thomas Howard's fleet was still fitting out in London, three of the frigates reaches Cascais at the mouth of the Tagus and the fourth, which had been separated from her consorts in a storm, arrived at San Lucar a week later. They were carrying the treasure of the Indies, five or six million pesos in gold and silver, about one and a half million pounds sterling — a simply colossal amount of money in the late sixteenth century. Lord Thomas Howard and his fleet heard this disheartening news as they cruised off Cape St Vincent, as Gawdy reports with some exaggeration. 'There is all ready four sayle come home to Snt. Lucers [San Lucar] in Andolusia laden with ten thousand millions six weekes before our comminge.'[18] Was it worth while continuing the voyage if so much treasure was already safe in Spain?

However, the King of Spain's treasure was not the only attraction of a summer cruise in the waters of the Azores. There was, for instance, the possibility of capturing one of the huge Portuguese carracks which sailed via the Azores on their way home to Lisbon from Goa in India. Drake had captured one of these in 1587, the *San Felipe* with a cargo worth over £100,000. And, in August 1592, an even more valuable carrack was to be captured in the islands, the *Madre de Deus*. She was to cause a sensation when she was brought safely home to port in Dartmouth. Her cargo of pepper, spices and Asian textiles was valued at £141,200 by merchants in London, but she was said to be carrying a further £100,000 or even £250,000 in jewels and precious stones, most of which were looted by the men on the spot when she surrendered after a long and bloody fight. Boxes and chests on deck had been plundered and even the cargo in the hold had been ransacked, quite contrary to the rules of the privateering game which forbade sailors from looting the cargo. Details of some of this loot have survived and they make one realize just why English seafarers endured the hardships of a privateering voyage — diamonds, pearls, rubies, sapphires, 'an emerald made in the form of a cross three inches in length', 'two great crosses and one other great jewel of diamonds which the Viceroy sent for a present to the King'. No wonder that the mariners refused to give up such marvels to their aristocratic employers.[19]

And even if neither a great Portuguese carrack nor the King of Spain's treasure was seized, there was still plenty more to be taken from the ships of the Spanish West Indian fleets. Even without the 'treasure', these ships were still very valuable, though one must discount the £20 million estimate of their worth which was being bandied about in England. Sir Richard Grenville himself had captured the vice-admiral of the Santo Domingo fleet in 1585, a prize that was no treasure ship and yet her cargo of 'sugar, hides, spices and some quantity of gold, silver and pearl' was valued at 40,000 ducats or about £14,000 or £15,000. A similarly valuable cargo on board a ship from Mexico was seized in 1589 by English corsairs cruising off the island of Fayal in the Azores. The captain of the Spanish ship said that she was carrying '16,000 ducketts in realls of plate in four chests and 17 baggs and more 12,000 ducketts in 21 baggs, besides 13 barres of silver plate, five chaines of gold, many ringes, braceletts and jewells, 270 chests of silke and other China commodities'.[20] Only ten or so ships like this would produce prizes worth as much as a *Madre de Deus*.

Early May was too soon to expect the fleets from the West Indies, but it was still worth while covering as much sea as possible to discover potential prizes. The English fleet stretched out in a very wide line as they sailed on towards the Azores, 'each ship two leagues at the least distance from another', just close enough to make certain that they could see each other from the mastheads. Signalling at sea was as yet rudimentary, but sufficient for the purpose: 'All the ships shall be careful to keep a man in the head of the topmast; and he that spies a sail shall shoot off a piece that way the sail bears and strike his topsail; and so many sails as he spies, so many times to strike his topsail.'

There were few topsails struck on this voyage for the ocean was largely empty and the men in Lord Thomas Howard's fleet were frustrated, 'the most of us like Lyons that have been allmost famished for want of prey'. And so they sailed on, every morning spreading out to search the sea and every evening coming close together again

with friendly salutations and gratulations one to an other, which they terme by the name of hayling; a ceremonie done solemnly and in verie good order, with sound of trumpets and noyse of cheerfull voyces: and in such sort performed as was no small encouragement one to the other, beside a true report of all such accidents as had happened in their squadrons.[21]

On two such evenings, there was a respite from the reports of an otherwise empty sea as two Spanish ships were encountered which proved valuable for the information in the letters they carried rather than for their cargo. Half-way between Cape St Vincent and the islands, they 'sonke a carvell, where we only saved three score jarrs of oyle, the men and a bushell of letters which they carried of intelligence to the islands to meet with the fleets coming home', i.e. letters from Spain to the Azores. And then, on Sunday 19 May, some 200 miles from the island of Santa Maria, they captured a ship travelling the other way, *La Concepción*, a small advice boat from Havana. Now they would be able to find out what was happening in the West Indies.[22]

CHAPTER SIX

IN THE WEST INDIES

The King of Spain's treasure comes unto him
as our salads to us — when we have eat all,
we fetch more out of our gardens; so doth he
fetch his treasure out of the ground after
spending all that is coined.[1]

'LEAVE THAT WRETCHED country, because it is only for people who have a lot of money,' wrote a young Spanish tailor in Mexico to his cousin in Spain. 'Here, no matter how poor a man may be, he never lacks a horse to ride and food to eat.'[2] The tailor's letter has the familiar ring of emigrants' letters back home across the ages, evoking a new life in a new world where those who had once been poor in Europe could eat, drink and get rich, where privilege went with a white skin and even a tailor could ride a horse like a gentleman.

The driving force of this utopia was the flood of silver which poured out of the ground in the remotest and most desolate parts of the Spanish American Empire, Zacatecas and Guanajuato in wild Indian country in Mexico and above all from the great silver mountain of Potosí in present-day Bolivia. Silver output rose higher and higher as the sixteenth century continued, to reach a peak in the early 1590s. While the Indian miners laboured, white men schemed and fought to get some of this American silver for themselves.

Some acquired the silver directly in the grim world of the mines, men like the Basque Nicolás de Guevara who went up to Potosí in 1581. Guevara, like most immigrants, planned to go home one day a rich man. 'I have or am gaining a great store of ore to process,' he wrote in 1595, 'and if it yields well, with the Lord's aid, I mean to go back to Spain within three years.'[3] But most Spanish Americans acquired their silver indirectly; they were administrators and churchmen who gathered in the fruits of office and devotion; they were the masters of the great *encomiendas* which provided food for the cities and the mines; they supplied services like the young tailor we met earlier; they acted as agents for the merchant houses of Seville who ensured the flow of European goods so eagerly demanded in America — clothes, textiles, furniture, even the basics of the Spanish kitchen such as wheat, wine and olive oil. And finally there was the King of Spain himself who garnered the most silver of all by taking a fifth of the output of the mines, the royal quint, a fundamental contribution to the funds enabling him to wage war.

Spanish policy in the Atlantic and in America was dominated by the absolute necessity of ensuring that this flow of silver got back to Spain intact, safe from the double threat of shipwreck and corsairs. The first stage had been to provide mutual protection through a fleet system whose timetable was designed to avoid sailing in the winter and during the hurricane season. Each year, one fleet left Spain sometime between April and early July for Mexico, taking with it the ships going to Puerto Rico, Santo Domingo, Cuba and Honduras as well as those going the whole way to Vera Cruz, the port of Mexico. Another fleet sailed from Spain along the Spanish Main to Cartagena in Colombia and on to Nombre de Dios, the fever-ridden port which was the terminus of the silver coming from Peru. These two fleets wintered in America, discharging and selling their European cargoes and gradually amassing their return cargoes. In terms of bulk, most of these were supplied from within the Caribbean — sugar, tobacco, ginger, indigo, hides, dyewoods and drugs. In value, however, over ninety-five per cent of return cargoes consisted of silver coins and bullion, silver which belonged to merchants and returning emigrants and to the King. When their ladings were complete, the two fleets converged on Havana sometime in the spring or early summer, as did other smaller fleets from the islands and from Honduras, ready for the combined fleets to sail together for Spain before September so as not to tempt God by sailing during the hurricane season.

Each fleet was normally convoyed by two well-gunned galleons and there was also a squadron of warships called the India Guard which provided protection between Cape St Vincent and the Canaries on the way out and between the Azores and Cape St Vincent on the way home, and sometimes accompanied the fleets the whole way to the West Indies. These galleons were financed by a tax on shippers called the *averia* whose incidence had risen considerably since the beginning of the war with England. This fleet system, with its strict timetable and endless rules, was not always followed as rigidly as the bureaucrats in Spain would have liked. It was, however, usually followed in its basic outlines and for the most part had been very successful. Fleets were sometimes unlucky with the weather or were delayed so long in American ports that they sailed in the hurricane season, with the result that there were many shipwrecks; stragglers were sometimes picked up by corsairs; but, despite ever-increasing numbers of ships in the fleets, the great majority successfully made the 8,000-mile round trip and the King and the Spanish merchants eventually got their silver.[4]

Defence of the fleets was remarkably successful, but little was done to protect the settlements in the Indies, a fact grimly exposed by raids made by the corsairs and especially by the great raids led by Drake in 1585 and 1586 when the cities of Santo Domingo and Cartagena were captured with embarrassing ease. Spanish reaction to this affront was fairly rapid, but cost determined that defence would be concentrated on the key-points ensuring the safety of the silver on its passage back to Spain. The rest of the Spanish Caribbean was left to its own resources to combat the rising tide of corsairs.[5]

For defence by sea, the Spanish relied on small ships operating in coastguard squadrons and on galleys, these oared fighting vessels being assigned to Santo Domingo, Puerto Rico, Cartagena and Havana. On land, the response was more impressive as, from the late 1580s, a great building programme began and walls, forts and castles rose from the ground and from the sea in such major ports as Havana, Vera Cruz, Cartagena, and Nombre de Dios. But, outside these favoured centres, there was no defence at all and the coastal populations were continually raided by corsairs, sometimes several times in the same year.

Convoys and castles made it harder for corsairs to capture ships or to raid the major ports, but the most effective Spanish innovation circumvented the lumbering fleets and their timetables altogether. This was the 'light armada' of *fregatas* or *zabras*, fast and well-armed ships such as those which slipped

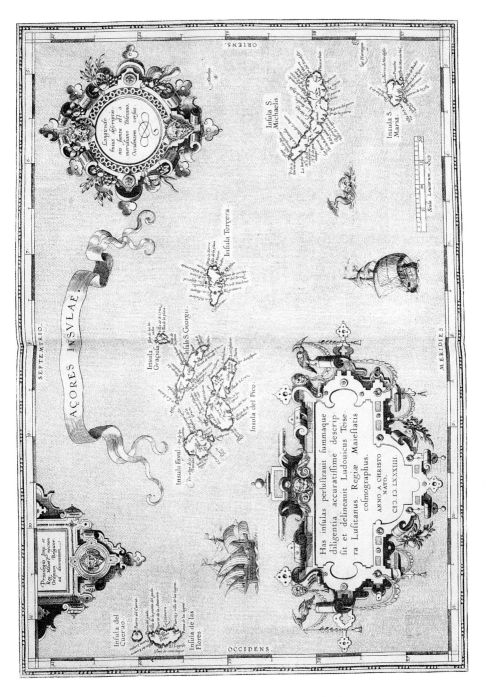

PLATE 5 *Map of the Azores by Abrahamus Ortelius,*
1584.

PLATE 6 *Queen Elizabeth by Isaac Olivier.*

PLATE 7 *Philip II of Spain by Hieronymus Wise, 1586.*

PLATE 8 *Detail from 'A Storm at Sea' by Jan Porcellis.*

into Cascais and San Lucar in March 1591 with five or six million pesos in gold and silver. These frigates, which only carried treasure and a few other items of high value and low bulk such as cochineal, had been immensely frustrating both for the corsairs in the West Indies and for successive fleets, such as that of Lord Thomas Howard, which had sought to capture the King of Spain's treasure in the Azores or in Spanish home waters. No English ship had as much as laid a gun on these swift *fregatas* which in every year since 1588 had brought home safely to Spain most of that ninety-five per cent of all American imports represented by silver. Most, but not all, since many merchants and other individuals ignored the royal orders to ship silver and other treasure on the *fregatas*. Some had neglected to pay the royal quint and so of necessity had to conceal their treasure. Others concealed it to avoid payment of the *averia* which was exceptionally heavy on the *fregatas*. Others preferred to keep really valuable treasure, such as gold chains and jewels, on their person. As a result, there was still quite a bit of treasure on the fleets which were to sail in 1591, a fact revealed to the English by Antonio de Ribero, part-owner of one of the ships in the fleet. 'There might be,' he reported, 'a myllion of gold secretly conveyed aboard.'[6]

It was, then, not just sugar and hides and other such mundane cargoes which had attracted the swarm of corsairs who were buzzing round the honey-pot of Havana in the early summer of 1591. Some of these were French Huguenots, but the majority were Englishmen, with eleven ships in all including the ships of John Watts which had deserted Lord Thomas Howard off the coast of Spain. Most of these men had cruised in the West Indies before, many of them several times, and they knew the coasts and the habits of the Spanish garrisons and fleets almost as well as did the Spaniards themselves. They were a rough lot, given to dissension, fighting over their spoils and heavy drinking, but they were dedicated to their work. They hung around the approaches to Havana with total impunity, infuriating the governor, Juan de Texeda, by sailing right into the mouth of the harbour shouting drunken insults and sending him 'love messages and compliments'. Well might he feel embarrassed, 'corralled' in his own city by such ruffians.[7]

There were many people in Havana to share Texeda's shame, for the city and its harbour were packed with men, women, children and ships —

nearly sixty in all — who were waiting to return to Spain. Some of these merchants, administrators, priests and returning emigrants had been waiting for over two years and nearly all of them had been in the Cuban city since the summer of 1590, eating and drinking their way through their American savings while worms ate through the ships' timbers and the humid tropical climate rotted rigging and sails. Delay had followed delay as a result of the Spanish belief that there was safety in numbers, a belief which led to orders that one delayed fleet should wait for the protection provided by another delayed fleet before setting sail for Spain and that no fleet should sail later than whatever was considered the last safe date to avoid the hurricanes.

And so a Mexican fleet had waited at Havana for a fleet from Cartagena under the command of Diego de la Ribera which had arrived on 19 July 1590, just four days too late to sail to Spain 'no later than 15 July'. And then, ironically, another messsage had arrived on the evening of 30 July that they should not sail later than 31 July. A *junta* (meeting) of fleet commanders and civil officers was hastily convened to consider whether it was possible to sail at one day's notice. Hardly surprisingly, they 'resolved that we winter here because the margin of time allowed us in which to get away is so short'.[8]

This decision caused consternation and despair in Madrid and in southern Spain whose merchants could now not hope to recover their investments until the summer of 1591 at the earliest. In England, it caused excitement at the thought of just how big the fleet of 1591 was now going to be. Meanwhile, the fleet commanders spent their Cuban winter squabbling with each other and getting their ships ready for the voyage, a task which was completed by late February when they received another message from Spain. This instructed them to wait in Havana for the arrival of yet another fleet under the command of Antonio Navarro de Prado which had arrived in Vera Cruz in a very battered condition on 29 October. The fleets in Cuba were also to wait, at least until 15 July, for the light armada of four *fregatas* commanded by Pedro Menendez Marquez which was to sail from Spain late in April 1591 to load silver in Cartagena and then return home via Havana. If Menendez did not arrive in time, the combined fleets were to sail for Spain, but were first to deposit all the gold and silver on board in the fort of Havana for Menendez to pick up in due course. The commanders in Havana digested their new instructions and settled down for another long wait while the season's crop of corsairs arrived to flaunt themselves at the harbour's mouth.

Early in May, Diego de la Ribera led a powerful squadron out of Havana to patrol off Cape San Antonio, the westernmost point of Cuba, in order to clear the seas of corsairs for the arrival of the fleet from Mexico. This assignment looked as though it might be fairly challenging with the arrival of the totally false information that a fleet of eighty English ships under the command of Sir Francis Drake had been seen in the waters of the Bahamas sailing west towards Havana. In fact, there was no Drake and the nearest English fleet was that of Lord Thomas Howard and Sir Richard Grenville which had not yet reached the Azores. Meanwhile, the corsairs who had been hanging around Havana prudently moved further east to harry shipping around Santo Domingo and Ribera was to see no enemies at all for over five weeks. His peaceful cruise was interrupted at dawn on 13 June when he fell in with four corsair ships, the *Hopewell*, the ship of John Watts which had been left behind when it ran aground in Falmouth, and the three ships set out by Sir George Carey — the 130-ton *Bark Burr* and her two minute consorts, the 35-ton *Swallow* and the 30-ton *Content*.[9]

Since Ribera's fleet at this moment consisted of four warships of over 600 tons each and two 100-ton *petachios*, one might have expected this squadron of minuscule English ships to run, but there was no sign of flight by the corsairs.[10] They thought their enemies were 'of the Cartagena fleet', a phrase which probably meant that they thought the Spaniards were the frigates of Menendez with several millions in silver, enough to give the crews of these four small ships the necessary courage to fight despite the odds, 'having made our prayers to almighty God'. Three of them attacked Ribera's flagship, an encounter which ended when the *Bark Burr* blew up after having been set on fire, while the *Hopewell* and the *Swallow* retired to a safe distance and took no further part in the fight.

This left the whole of Ribera's fleet with just one remaining enemy, the *Content*, a ship of 30 tons with one saker and four other small guns and just twenty-three men against a fleet of six ships whose combined tonnage was nearly 3,000 with guns to match and about 1,500 men. The story of her astonishing fight 'from seven in the morning till sunset' is an object lesson in Elizabethan naval warfare and shows just how difficult it was for the warships of the day to sink or capture an opponent, however small, who was prepared to put up a determined resistance.

Captain Nicolas Lisle of the *Content* opened the action by sailing up to the Spanish vice-admiral — over twenty times his size — and giving him 'a volley of muskets and our great ordinance'. This bold gesture was followed for the rest of the day by a long running fight with varying numbers of Spanish ships as the nimble *Content*, abandoned by her consorts, tried to get out of trouble. She sailed first one way and then another to avoid the guns of her pursuers who were often close enough to engage with her small guns and even with muskets, such martial activity being regularly interspersed with further prayers to almighty God.

Later in the day, the wind dropped and the men of the *Content* took to their oars 'that we might row to shore, and anker in shallow water where their great ships could not come nigh us, for other refuge had we none'. But this tactic simply led to one of the shallow-draught *petachios* being packed with extra men who themselves took to the oars to pursue the *Content* inshore. Prayer was effective at this point for, at the last moment, 'the Lord of his mercie did send us a fair gale of wind' which enabled the *Content* to outdistance her pursuers and sail off to safety. However, the respite was only brief as, towards evening, the two galleys of the Cuban Guard showed up and this time the *Content* really did have a fight on her hands.

The flag galley with 200 soldiers and sailors and 250 slave and convict oarsmen, some of them captured English corsairs, soon caught up with the *Content*. 'They bid us amaine [surrender] English dogs and came upon our quarter starboard; and giving us five cast pieces out of her prow, they sought to lay us aboard; but wee so galled them with our muskets that we put them from our quarter.' The galley was soon back, her oarsmen rowing up to the stern of the *Content* with such momentum that her beakhead burst open the timbers of Captain Lisle's cabin. Now was the moment of truth when the long bow-chasers of the galley should have been able to sink the little ship, which at this stage had only thirteen men to defend her, the other ten having taken prudent refuge in the hold. These bold thirteen gathered all the muskets they could find into the stern and fired down on the galley's gunners and on the soldiers in her prow who, sensing victory was at hand, were 'fighting with great spirit' — but not with quite such spirit as the men of the *Content*. 'Wee being resolute, so plyed them with our small shot that they could have no time to discharge their great ordinance: and when they began to approach, wee heaved into them a ball of fire, and by that means put them off: whereupon they once againe fell asterne.'

As night fell and the soldiers and sailors of the galley licked their wounds, they listened with amazement to the cockney crew of the *Content* singing 'the first part of the 25 Psalme, praising God for our safe deliverance', words which must have brought joy to the Englishmen on the galley's rowing benches.

Lift mine hart to thee, my God and guide most just:
Now suffer me to take no shame, for in thee doe I trust;
Let not my foes rejoyce, nor make a scorne of me
And let them not be overthrown that put their trust in thee.

God heard the prayer and sent a wind in the night which blew the *Content* safely away, her decks awash with cannon-balls, her sides and masts 'sowed thick with musket bullets', her sheets, tops and shrouds 'almost cut in sunder with their great and small shot' and, astonishingly, not a single man killed and only two wounded. These drunken, insolent corsairs, who turned to their 'Lutheran' God when they were in trouble, had lived to fight another day. The Spaniards, needless to say, made little mention in their report of the 'memorable fight' of the *Content*, though Pedro Alvarez, the captain of the flag galley, was later commended for conducting 'himself very creditably, like a good soldier'.[11]

The disappointed Ribera continued to cruise off Cape San Antonio for another ten days, but there was still no sign of the Mexican fleet nor of Menendez and the *fregatas* and, on 24 June, he sailed back into Havana Bay, his victuals exhausted. Menendez had in fact arrived in Cartagena by then and his *fregatas* were busy picking up the silver which had been stored there and in Nombre de Dios. However, grossly exaggerated rumours of a huge English presence in the Caribbean, and even of an English occupation of Havana, persuaded him to stay where he was and he did not venture out for Havana until the last week of August.

Meanwhile, Antonio Navarro and the Mexican fleet had been ready to sail from Vera Cruz, 'with yards across', ever since the middle of April but had been forced to remain at anchor by the non-arrival of the mule train with the King's gold and silver. This eventually turned up on 3 June and he set sail on the same day with twenty-two ships. The voyage from Vera Cruz to Havana was generally considered the worst part of the whole round trip, a thousand miles straight into the prevailing winds, though on this occasion the problem was lack of wind and 'the voyage was a little tiresome' as they crept through the appalling summer heat of the Gulf of Mexico to arrive in Havana nearly five weeks later on 6 July. Worse still, two stragglers were lost to the corsairs, the 400-ton *Joana* loaded with hides and the *Trinity* of Seville with over £20,000-worth of silver, cochineal and hides.[12]

This valuable prize persuaded most of the Englishmen that it was time to go home while the weather still remained fine. It had been a good season with prizes well up into double figures, including seven ships from a fleet of ten which had attempted vainly to get to Havana from Santo Domingo, some indication of the ineffectiveness of the Spanish coastguard and galley patrols. The Spaniards themselves took out their frustration on Juan Gayon, the pilot of the captured *Trinity*, whom the English had rather unkindly set ashore. Gayon, who for 'no known reason' had steered his ship away from the protection of the rest of the fleet, was arrested and prosecuted in Havana where he 'was sentenced to public disgrace and ten years on the rowers' bench in the galleys'. Navarro was none too happy with such a feeble sentence. 'If they had not taken the case out of my jurisdiction, I'd have hanged him.'[13]

Now, at last, everyone hoping to sail to Spain was in Havana except the unfortunate fleet from Santo Domingo and Menendez and his *fregatas*. As he had still not arrived by the long-awaited deadline of St James's Day, 15

July, Navarro carried out the instructions from Spain. Nearly five million pesos in treasure was unloaded from his ships and put under guard in the fort and, a couple of days later, the combined fleets set sail, a total of nearly eighty ships and many thousands of men, women and children who prepared themselves to run the gauntlet of the 3,000 miles of stormy sea and the two English fleets which lay between Cuba and the coast of Spain.[14]

The return voyage from America was nearly always unpleasant. Ships which might have been quite sound on the way out aged fast in tropical ports and soon began to leak at every seam. Every inch of space was crammed with the precious American cargo, even at the expense of defence and navigation, and there was little room left for the passengers who paid small fortunes for a few square feet of cramped deck space. Fresh food and water soon turned out to have been not so fresh, even when loaded, and were rotten or stale after a few weeks at sea, though not too stale for the armies of rats who roamed the decks. On one notorious voyage from Havana, more than 4,000 rats were killed before the ship reached the Azores, a welcome supplement to the diet of those who were not too squeamish. But most people were too busy being seasick to eat rats, as storms, rain and leaden skies made an unwelcome contrast to the balmy seas, the fireworks and fiestas, the pleasant days and nights spent speeding along before the north-east trades, some 1,500 miles further south, on the outward voyage. And this return voyage was not just unpleasant but also very dangerous, so that passengers might well fear that each day would be their last.

The voyagers protected themselves against such dangers with an ample supply of lucky charms and relics of saints and with a programme of religion even more intense than the prayers and psalms which rose aloft from the decks of a Protestant galleon. Even the foul-mouthed sailors joined in this devotion, men whom Cervantes described as heathen and inurbane whose favourite amusement was 'to watch the passengers being seasick'.[15] A Spanish traveller has described the routine:

> Our method was, at break of day we sang the *Te deum*. After sun-rising . . .
> four or five masses were said, and all the crew resorted to them: in the

afternoon the *Salve Regina* and Litany of our Lady was sung, then the Rosary was said by gangs, some miraculous stories were read, and there was some discourse of religious matters ... An hour after the *Angelus Domini*, a man went out at the hatch ... and having rung a little bell, in the saddest and most doleful voice that ever I heard, said, 'Death is certain, the Hour uncertain, the Judge severe. Woe unto thee who art slothful!' He rang the bell again, and praying for the souls departed, withdrew and all the crew repenting for their sins went to rest in the deepest silence.[16]

The combined fleets of 1591 faced bad weather almost from the moment they left Havana,[17] but such spiritual efforts were successful in wafting them through both the first and second of the great navigational dangers of the return voyage — the Straits of Florida, whose treacherous reefs and shoals had been the graveyard of innumerable Spanish ships, and the stormy waters of Bermuda. But these doomed fleets were not to enjoy divine protection for much longer. On 14 August, four weeks out of Havana, the wind 'changed suddenly to the north so that the sea coming out of the south-west and the wind at north, they were all in great extremity'. Two days later, the Mexican flagship under the command of Antonio Navarro and twelve other ships disappeared from sight. 'Everything possible was done to discover them but they could not be found.'

The remaining sixty-five or so ships continued their voyage through terrible weather under the leadership of Diego de la Ribera and of Navarro's vice-admiral, Aparicio de Arteaga. On 24 August

the wind blew strong from every quarter and raised a wild sea. It seemed like the tail-end of a hurricane. That night the wind blew from the north with great violence and the seas were very high. That night the flagship (where Diego de Ribera was) split and on the 25th, between eight and nine in the morning, went down within sight of many vessels unable to help. Over 200 persons were drowned, among them the general and the inspector and other persons of importance. Some 30 persons only were saved.

Ribera's ship was but the first of many of the rotten fleet which 'split' and foundered that day and during the seven continuous days of terrible storm that followed. Many men were transferred to other ships before their own went down, others were picked up from the sea or from where they lay clinging to the wreckage, but the loss was still appalling. Arteaga took command after the death of Ribera and, when the storm at last subsided, he counted his fleet. There were only forty-nine ships left — eleven had sunk before his eyes in the mid-Atlantic and some five or six more had vanished.

Meanwhile, Navarro with the rump of the fleet had marginally better fortune after his separation from his colleagues. In addition to the continuous storms, he had to face an added hazard when three English ships were discovered among his fleet and these corsairs continued to trail him and to snap at stragglers throughout his voyage. But, in the storm which took such terrible toll of the rest of the fleet, he lost only one ship, albeit a very important one — the vice-admiral of the fleet from Cartagena. All those on board were saved and distributed among the other twelve ships which continued their voyage towards the Azores, some days ahead of Arteaga and his forty-nine remaining ships. Nearly eighty ships had left Havana after their long delay; only sixty-one remained, battered and distressed, to face the fleet of Lord Thomas Howard and Sir Richard Grenville which awaited them so impatiently in the Azores. These sixty-one ships rolled along before the westerly winds of the North Atlantic, 'as helpless a mass of booty as any Admiral could wish to see sail into his hands'.[18]

CHAPTER SEVEN

ALARMS AND
EXCURSIONS

The life of an action by sea is to get
intelligence of an enemy, and to keep
the enemy from intelligence; for in that
case a man is armed and guarded to
encounter an enemy naked and unprovided.[1]

THE MANAGEMENT OF war was far from easy in a world where news
could travel no faster than a horse on land or a sailing ship at sea.
Even to discover where one's own forces were and what they were doing
might take a matter of weeks. To discover what the enemy was up to was
obviously even more difficult since it involved the collection, assessment
and analysis of a variety of usually conflicting and sometimes deliberately
misleading information. Such problems were then compounded by the fact
that the information, correct or not at the time of collection, might be
completely out of date by the time it reached London or Madrid. All this
meant that governments were generally nervous once they had committed
forces overseas and tended uncritically to believe exaggerated reports of the
hostile intentions of the enemy.

English intelligence relied on reports from commanders in the field or
at sea, on the interrogation of those captured aboard prizes or of sailors
and others who had recently been in or near Spanish territory, on letters
from persons living abroad who sought the favour of the government and
on a network of amateur and paid spies. Some of the results of this activity
have survived and the historian can sympathize with the problems of those
who had to interpret such intelligence.[2] There is, for instance, a letter in
the Public Record Office dated 3 December 1590 from 'a well-willer of Her
Majesty' in Andalucia. This gives remarkably accurate information about

the plans of the Spanish navy and about the timetable to be adopted by the fleets returning from the Indies in the summer of 1591. It also predicts almost to the day the date on which the light armada of *fregatas* would reach Spain from Havana and offers a fairly realistic plan to capture them and the five or six million pesos of treasure that they were carrying. Since the letter gave three months' notice of the arrival of the *fregatas*, the patriotic historian cannot help but feel a terrible sense of frustration that the English took no notice of such superb intelligence. But they, of course, were not to know that this one letter among so many correctly predicted Spanish naval policy for the next eight months.[3]

Instead, the English relied mainly on their two agents in place in south-west France, the Frenchman Chateaumartin in Bayonne and Edmund Palmer in St Jean-de-Luz. Neither of these men was totally reliable and both were easily suborned by Don Juan Velazquez, the Governor of Guipuzcoa, who managed a network of spies and double agents and reported regularly to King Philip. Chateaumartin was already a double agent in 1591, a fact discovered by the English in the following year when they learned that he was receiving 100 crowns a month from Philip II in addition to the 1,000 crowns a year that he was paid by Queen Elizabeth. Palmer was constantly under suspicion because of his personal character. He drank too much, was married to a Spanish woman, was so indiscreet in his language against the King of Spain and Spaniards that 'they watched to lay hold of him' and was 'over familiar with merchants, a kind of people no way to be trusted and mortal foes to gentle blood'. A few years later, he too was taking money from Don Juan Velazquez to reveal 'all the secrets of England, as well as the many spies there are in Spain'.[4] In spite of this duplicity, these two agents provided reasonably accurate information for their English masters (as well as for their Spanish ones), and were of course well placed to report on activity in the ports of northern Spain. Palmer, for instance, had a man in Valladolid and two others keeping an eye on every Spanish harbour from Fuenterrabia and Pasajes just over the border from St Jean-de-Luz to the twin naval bases of Ferrol and Corunna in the extreme north-west of Galicia.[5]

This was dangerous work, but Palmer's sub-agents were able to provide a flow of fairly accurate information on the build-up of Spanish naval forces and on the raising of an alarmingly large number of soldiers. They wrote of new ships being built and launched, of the dispatch of masts, cables, munitions and ship's biscuit. Gradually, through the spring and early summer of 1591, ships were fitted out and reported moving along the coast to converge on the port of Ferrol. It soon became only too apparent that, for the first time since the defeat of the Armada in 1588, the Spanish navy would be going to sea in real strength sometime in the summer.

The problem facing Lord Burghley and other English ministers was to determine the destination of these ships and men. Should they believe an alarmist report from Lisbon via Dublin that 500 ships were planning to invade England?[6] Or should they believe Palmer and Chateaumartin who inclined to the view that most of these ships and men were destined to reinforce the Spanish expeditionary force in Brittany, leaving a comparatively small fleet to form the India Guard and 'waft home' the treasure fleets from the Azores? And when would these treasure fleets arrive — vital information to be relayed to Lord Thomas Howard and Sir Richard Grenville? Some people said they would be leaving Havana in April, some in May, some in June, but none of the reports picked up the news that 15 July was to be the deadline for leaving Havana, a fact known in Spain since December and in Havana since late February. The confusion of information grew greater as the season advanced and there were more ships at sea to provide it, such as the fleet of the Earl of Cumberland which at last set sail for the coast of Spain in May. By then the English had received conflicting reports that the Spanish fleet intended to invade England or Ireland, to occupy the Isle of Wight, the Channel Islands or the Scillies, to reinforce Brittany or the Netherlands. Any one of these reports, or none of them, might be true.

It was all very confusing and indeed alarming for an English government which had already committed several of its best ships to the Azores. What was to be done? In the end, it was decided to try to cover all eventualities. The most pressing danger seemed to be in Brittany from where it was feared a powerful Spanish army and their French allies of the Catholic League might move out to link up with the Duke of Parma's army on the borders of the Low Countries and then drive England's ally, Henry IV, out of the north of France. This would leave the whole of the French coast of the Channel in Spanish or Leaguer hands, a very dangerous state of affairs. Plans for an English expedition to Brittany which had been agreed in principle in the previous winter now acquired a greater urgency and Sir John Norris eventually arrived there with 3,000 men early in May. In late July and August, another expeditionary force under the Earl of Essex landed in Dieppe to assist King Henry IV of France in his projected siege of Rouen. Neither of these English armies achieved any great success, but the dispatch of some 8,000 English soldiers overseas at a time when the government was worried about invasion is some indication of the importance that French affairs bore in English minds in the summer of 1591.

Nearer home, the threat of invasion was taken seriously. Orders were sent to lords lieutenant to get their trained bands prepared and to man the beacons which had remained in readiness since Armada year. Particular attention was paid to the apparently threatened Isle of Wight and to the report that a fleet of twenty (or was it thirty-five?) Spanish ships was keeping the seas between Ushant and Scilly; indeed it was believed by many that the Spaniards had actually occupied the Scilly Isles. All this was totally untrue, but the rumours caused shivers in London and action was taken accordingly.

Sir Henry Palmer was sent in April with two galleons of the Channel Guard to reinforce the small force patrolling the western approaches to the Channel and was later joined by another two of the Queen's ships. Other ships were made ready in Portsmouth for immediate service. In May, the Earl of Cumberland was ordered to 'employ himself against the Spaniards', something he was already trying to do, and Sir Walter Raleigh was sent to Plymouth 'to take up ships and men there to save Silley if it be not taken and to defend ye coast of Cornwall and Devon'. He was also to send a pinnace to the Azores to warn Lord Thomas Howard of these dangerous new Spanish activities.[7]

Meanwhile, there were worries about Lord Thomas himself. His ships had received victuals for only four months and these would long be exhausted if the treasure fleets did not arrive until September or October, as was now expected. There were also growing fears that his fleet might not be strong enough to defend itself against the India Guard fitting out in Ferrol or even against the warships escorting the treasure fleets from Havana, which were reported quite erroneously to be twenty-two or twenty-three in number 'soe as it is likely they come very stronglie'. In fact, there was less than a third of this number and, as we have seen, two of these were to end their voyage at the bottom of the Atlantic and so were unlikely to cause Lord Thomas much of a problem.[8]

Such anxieties led to a flurry of orders and activity in late May and June.[9] Two months' further victuals for Lord Thomas Howard's fleet were gathered together and shipped on four flyboats which were escorted to the Azores by the 500-ton *Golden Lion* and the 300-ton *Foresight* 'for his better strength and to wafte the vyttels'. A concerted effort was also made to strengthen Howard's fleet by attempting to find more privateers to join him. The City of London responded loyally, or with a keen sense of the possible profits, and eventually fitted out six powerful privateer ships of between 250 and 400 tons and two pinnaces, though they did not leave London until 21 July and were then weatherbound in Plymouth until 17 August.

Outside London, however, there was little enthusiasm shown for a voyage to the Azores. A request to the Dutch to fit out 'ten good shippes, the least to be of the burden of 100 tonnes', to serve under Lord Thomas and so gain 'a masse of treasure' fell on deaf ears, hardly surprisingly since they had no warships of that tonnage and what ships they did have were active elsewhere. A round robin to the English ports to provide at least one ship each of over 100 tons was also almost completely unsuccessful. One after the other, their spokesmen regretfully declined the invitation, pleading that they had no ships of that size or if they had that they were already engaged elsewhere, professing poverty or a dearth of sailors because these had already been pressed by Howard or by the Earl of Cumberland. Of all the ports from Newcastle to Bristol, the only one to respond positively was Weymouth which offered the 120-ton *White Lion*, 'at present in the river of Thames, very sufficient and fit for the same service'. In the absence of any further reinforcements, Lord Thomas was therefore going to have to do the best he could with the forces already at his disposal and he was no doubt pleased to receive a letter from the Queen dated 2 July: 'And thus with our prayer to the Allmighty for your safe and happy retourne to our presence, wee commit you to his good protection.'[10]

While the English spent May and June in a state of jitters, if not downright panic, the Spaniards were of course not idle in their preparations. Communications were an even greater problem for the Spanish, who needed to co-ordinate activities and information throughout the known world and especially between America, Spain and Flanders. Distance alone made for lengthy delays and hence inaccuracies in the passage of information and these were compounded by the capture of advice boats by corsairs. The Spaniards went to great lengths to combat these problems. In December 1590, for instance, no fewer than seven small ships of advice sailed separately from Seville to the Indies in order to ensure that at least one of them got there safely with the King's instructions.[11]

Such delays and dangers could cause serious problems in planning a campaign, but the plans themselves seem to have been based on more accurate information than was available to the English. Indeed, King Philip had a powerful reputation both for the collection of intelligence and for its interpretation and was said to know the whereabouts and future plans of every English ship. This no doubt exaggerated the King's clairvoyance, but his spies in London certainly kept him well informed. He had known at a very early stage of the plan to send a fleet to the Azores and also that this fleet was unlikely to sail before April, information which determined the timing of the sailing of the light armada of *fregatas* which reached Spain in early March. The King knew too that Howard was to be supplied with only four months' victuals, knowledge which played an important part in the decision to delay the sailing of the combined fleets from Havana so that they would arrive in the Azores after Howard's provisions had been exhausted.

As the campaigning season got under way, the King now needed to know in more detail the size and strength of Howard's fleet and the exact timing of its movements. He also needed to know when and with how many men Sir John Norris was going to sail to Brittany. The Spanish information system went into action. The first informants were a Dutchman who had sailed from London on 1 April and arrived in Setubal near Lisbon on 19 April and Antonio de Sousa, a native of Lisbon who had been held captive in London and then released, returning to his native land on 24 April. Both men reported Howard's departure from the Thames and de Sousa was able to report his departure from Plymouth as well. He did however underestimate the strength of the English fleet, saying that there were only two galleons of the Queen.[12]

Further information was provided by Captain Martín de Oleaga who arrived in Santander on 20 May after cruising with a squadron of five *zabras* in the Bristol Channel and off the coast of Cornwall '*para tomar lingua*' — to get news. They captured and took prisoners from three English merchantmen, including a coal boat trading between Swansea and Falmouth. At dead of night, a raiding party of twenty-five men was also landed on the Cornish coast. They marched inland and knocked up a house in a village a few miles from Falmouth. One householder lost his life as he bravely tried to defend himself against this alarming nocturnal visitation, but one of his fellow villagers was seized and taken back aboard to join the prisoners from the merchantmen. They were interrogated with the aid of John of Galway, an Irishman living in Santander who acted as interpreter. What degree of physical persuasion was required, we do not know, but the prisoners certainly talked and revealed well-informed knowledge of such matters as the movements of Sir John Norris, the dispositions of the English fleet and the plans for the coming privateering season. If Cornish villagers and seamen from Welsh coal boats knew such things, one must assume that English naval security was virtually nil.[13]

The Spanish authorities continued to receive further information regarding Lord Thomas Howard's progress. This was not too difficult. If Philip Gawdy was able to see 'one of the Kinges houses' as he sailed past Cascais, it is not surprising that the watchers on the Portuguese coast could see and count the English fleet. They noticed too when Lord Thomas at last headed out to sea in the direction of the Azores. More was learned of the strength of the fleet from a letter written on 6 July by the Conde de Fuentes, the Captain-General of Portugal. He had cross-questioned a sailor whom the English had captured on board the advice ship *Concepción* and subsequently released. This anonymous informant had certainly kept his eyes open and was able to report fairly accurately the tonnage and the number of guns and men in most of the ships of Lord Thomas's fleet.[14]

The sailor had also had the opportunity to make similar observations of the fleet of the Earl of Cumberland which were added to a mass of information already collected on the privateering earl's activities. These had in fact been none too successful. He had sailed from England in May with seven ships and 'being arrived on the Spanish coast it was his hap to take three ships at several times, one with wine, which he unloaded and divided amongst his fleet, and two with sugars'. Then things began to go seriously wrong. One of the sugar prizes sprang a leak and had to be abandoned. The other was forced into Corunna by bad weather, 'where they rendered themselves to the enemy's mercy'. Finally, one of Cumberland's own ships with 14 guns and 150 men, together with two smaller ships, were surprised in calm weather off the Berlingas Islands by a squadron of five galleys led by Don Francisco Coloma.

The English ships were commanded by Captain William Monson, later to be a famous name in English naval circles. However, on this occasion, Monson, his men and his ships were captured after what the English reported as 'a long and bloody fight', though the Spaniards stressed the ease of their victory with only two men killed and a few wounded. Normally, captured corsairs could expect such harsh punishment as being consigned to the rowing benches of the galleys, but Captain Monson reported with surprise that 'the ordinary men were treated with more courtesy than they had been from the beginning of the war.' Such kind treatment was the result of a letter sent to Coloma by the Earl of Cumberland in which he promised to treat well the prisoners that he himself had taken if Coloma would do the same, a promise which seems to have been honoured by both sides. But this was just about the only honour that Cumberland achieved that summer and, in August, he decided to curtail his campaign and return to England, 'considering the disasters that thus befel him'.[15]

Fairly accurate information on the movements of the English fleets was of course paralleled by intelligence just as spurious as anything received by Lord Burghley in London. Almost inevitably, there were several reports that Sir Francis Drake was ready to go to sea for some great exploit, though one informant reported more accurately and prosaically that Drake had earned 'great fame amongst the local population' for bringing a new fresh-water supply to Plymouth. There was also a lot of confusion about English shipping movements in the Bay of Biscay with reports of fleets about to seize Lisbon or some other port, which caused the same sort of consternation as the English reports that the Spaniards had captured the Scillies. Exciting news arrived from Brussels in early July that the whole of Lord Thomas Howard's fleet had been captured by fifteen galleys 'without a fight' in the Straits of Gibraltar.[16] Such reports had to be sifted carefully for the grain of truth they might contain. But on the main issues the Spanish authorities were well informed. They probably thought that Lord Thomas Howard's fleet was rather smaller and weaker than it actually was and that the Earl of Cumberland's was rather stronger, but overall their information was remarkably good as they continued their preparations in Ferrol for the summer's naval campaign.

CHAPTER EIGHT

SPANISH SHIPS OF WAR AT SEA

Cuanto el Rey debe al que
sirve en la mar bravia.[1]

How much the King owes to those
who serve him on the savage sea.

K ING PHILIP OF SPAIN may have wept when first he heard of the terrible losses of the 'Invincible' Armada of 1588, but his tears soon turned to stoical acceptance of God's will and a determination that an even more powerful armada should replace the one so sadly battered by 'the winds and by the fortune of the sea'. The great English victory thus ironically resulted in the creation of a permanent Spanish navy in the Atlantic and not in its eclipse. Spain had had no real high seas navy at all before the 1580s and had relied in times of need on ships that were chartered or commandeered from private shipowners. There had then been a slow build-up in the 1580s, which began with Philip's acquisition of the galleons of Portugal when he became king of that country, but the number of royal ships was still quite small in 1588. During the 1590s, however, King Philip was to have as the main fighting heart of his fleet some twenty or thirty royal galleons, more than were usually available to Queen Elizabeth, and these could be augmented to much greater numbers by taking private ships into the fleet.[2]

The core of the fleet of 1591 was provided by the galleons which had survived the disasters of the Armada three years earlier, those ships Sir Francis Drake had so unwisely allowed to remain safely at their moorings in Santander in 1589. As the English agent Edmund Palmer wrote from St Jean-de-Luz:

If Sir Francis had gone to Santander . . . he had done such a service as never subject had done. For with twelve sail of his ships he might have destroyed all the forces which the Spaniards had there, which was the whole strength of the country by sea. There they did ride all unrigged and their ordnance on the shore and some twenty men only in a ship to keep them.[3]

This potential naval strength was soon to become a real one and was drawn mainly from the squadron of Castile which lost only one galleon in the Armada campaign and from the squadron inherited from Portugal. Between them, these two squadrons provided eleven royal galleons for the campaign of 1591, including the 1,000-ton *San Martín*, the flagship of the Duke of Medina Sidonia in 1588. The normal function of the galleons of Castile was to act as the India Guard and so, like the Portuguese galleons, they were built to be able to withstand the weather of the Atlantic, one reason for their relatively high survival rate in Armada year.

To reinforce this core of royal galleons, King Philip began a massive building programme to replace the ships that had been lost with new and better ones. Most of this building took place in the Basque yards of northern Spain and the main focus of pride was the construction of six fine new galleons in Santander and six in Bilbao — the famous Twelve Apostles. These were to be built along 'English' lines, though they were to be considerably larger than the galleons of the *Revenge* type, from 750 to 1,500 tons, figures which need to be reduced by ten or twenty per cent for comparison with English tonnages. Other smaller ships were also being built for the King, and the years since the Armada had seen unparalleled activity in northern Spain as officers roamed the oak forests to mark trees for felling and craftsmen and labourers worked away with adze and saw under the supervision of royal experts in the yards.[4] Meanwhile, private shipowners and shipbuilders were encouraged to build warships of their own, both for service under contract in the royal fleet and as privateers. English fleets had sailed with almost no challenge from the Spaniards in 1589 and 1590, but it was clear that this was unlikely to be true in 1591.

The English agent Chateaumartin sent a man into northern Spain early in March who reported that all was quiet and all Spanish ships disarmed. But, thenceforward, there was to be a crescendo of activity, in Ferrol where the royal fleet was assembling and in every yard and harbour along the coast, at Pasajes, Portugalete, Bilbao and Santander, where shipwrights and riggers laboured to get old ships fitted out or new ships built for the season's campaign. The English agents took particular interest in the progress of the Twelve Apostles. In January, these were little more than bare hulls with no masts or cables. But, in the weeks that followed, merchantmen were constantly arriving with the necessary stores and the work pressed ahead so fast that by mid-April it was reported that 'the six great ships of Bilbao and the six of Santander were launched and masted', no doubt with appropriate ritual for such a solemn and auspicious moment in Spanish naval history. Three Apostles from each port were to be prepared speedily to join the fleet in Ferrol.[5] And so the work went on, the laggards stirred into action by letter after letter from King Philip, a torrent of royal correspondence stilled only temporarily in April and May when the King was reported to be very ill with gout, fever and pain in his neck, so ill indeed that they were taking bets in Zeeland on his life. But King Philip was not to die just yet and he was soon back at his desk in El Escorial.

The man at the centre of the great web of activity that was northern Spain was the captain-general of the royal fleet, Don Alonso de Bazán, one of those unfortunate historical figures who are always introduced by reference to a more famous relative. Don Alonso is thus known as the brother of Don Alvaro de Bazán, Marqués of Santa Cruz, one of the most famous men in Spanish naval history — hero of Lepanto, conqueror of the Azores, original commander and architect of the plan for the Spanish Armada, a plan which might have led to different results had he not died of typhus in February 1588.[6] Don Alonso could only suffer by comparison with such a man, despite his own long career on land and at sea, a total of thirty-eight years in the King's service. His strengths lay more in planning and theory than in bold exploits and action at sea. He was a distinguished writer on naval affairs, a ship designer who was credited with the invention of the strong and speedy frigates and *zabras* which carried the American treasure so successfully home from 1588, and he was 'highly esteemed and very well versed in business matters'. It was business which concerned him in his letters to the King as he fretted about the fitting-out of his fleet. This task reveals him as a sensible, practical and careful man, but one who was constantly worrying and complaining and blaming other people for the delays which left his fleet still anchored in the harbour of Ferrol as each successive deadline set by King Philip expired.[7]

There was a shortage of everything. Where were the sailors to come from in a country that had been so 'destroyed for mariners' by the loss of life in 1588, a country where 'cobblers, tinkers and shoemakers, and horse boys and labourers' had to be pressed into the fighting ships? And where were the veteran infantry to fight on those ships? There were not even enough masters and pilots, a problem which Bazán solved by offering to double their pay. But soon Don Alonso was worrying about something else. He had scoured the north of Spain without success for chaplains to serve in the fleet and begged the King to find him some elsewhere, 'because Your Highness knows the distress that people feel upon embarking when they discover that there is no one to whom they can confess in case of necessity'.[8]

Human problems were matched by material ones. There was not enough biscuit or wine or cables or masts or a thousand other things. Above all, there were not enough guns for a navy which had left so many among the rocks and sands of the Irish coast in 1588. The resources of the huge Spanish Empire were combed to try to produce more guns to replace them. Royal imports of pepper from Sumatra and India were bartered in Lisbon for Hungarian copper which in turn was delivered to the King's German gun-founder. But it was not enough. The gun foundries could not match the productivity of the shipyards and this serious problem was not to be solved, despite pleas to have guns sent from the foundries of Lisbon and Andalucia, despite the clandestine dispatch of English guns which arrived from Lubeck, Hamburg and other neutral ports concealed under cargoes of coal. When the fleet did finally set sail, Don Alonso claimed that there were still only half as many guns as necessary.[9]

Nevertheless, progress was made, but it was slow progress as May, June and half July went by and the fleet was not yet ready for sea, despite reiterated commands from the King to hurry up and reiterated promises from Bazán that he would not delay a single day or even a single hour if only

. . . whatever it was that was still missing would turn up. Slowly, the ships in Ferrol rose in numbers — thirty-two, then forty, then fifty, reported the English agents. Masts, cables and other gear arrived from all over Europe, despite the efforts of English corsairs to do a Drake and capture them on the way. Two thousand suits of clothing specially ordered by the King were delivered, complete with black felt sombreros. Sailors were found, though they were reported to be discontented because they had not received their pay. Veteran soldiers marched or rode in and their numbers were made up by scouring the towns and villages of Galicia and 'taking every fifth man as usual'. Even chaplains were found.[10]

Meanwhile, the provisions for the thousands of men who were to sail with the armada began to accumulate. These seem to have been more varied and of better quality than those provided for the English fleet — wheaten ship's biscuit, salt pork, salt beef, salt cod, sardines and tunny, cheese, chick-peas, rice and wine — sufficient for nineteen meat days, nine fish days and three cheese days a month. The American historian Carla Rahn Phillips has analysed the nutritional content of the victuals provided for Spanish royal fleets and has found that, though boring and unappetizing, they offered a healthy diet, more than adequate for the hard labour of shipboard life. They also contained most of the nutrients needed to maintain human efficiency, except retinol, which 'could have led to night blindness', and vitamin C. Despite this deficiency in their rations, Spanish seamen never suffered so seriously from scurvy as the English, probably because of immunities arising from their normal diet of citrus fruit, onions, peppers and garlic.[11]

On 27 May, there was joy in Ferrol as General Antonio de Urquiola arrived with the three Apostles which had been built in Santander, including the mighty 1,500-ton *San Pablo* which was to replace *San Martín* as the *capitana real* or flagship of the fleet. The new galleons were still short of some of their equipment and grievously short of artillery, but they appeared magnificent to those who watched them sail in. 'Experts say,' reported Don Alonso to the King, 'they are amongst the finest ships that they have ever seen, powerful, fast and making very little water.' There was, however, still no news of Don Martín de Bertendona who was to bring the other three Apostles from Bilbao and there was to be no news of him for weeks. He

THE SPANISH FLEET OF 1591

	TONS	GUNS
SQUADRON OF THE CAPTAIN-GENERAL ALONSO DE BAZÁN		
*Galleon San Pablo (Apostle — flagship)	1,480	42
*Galleon San Martín de Portugal	1,000	32
*Galleon San Felipe (Apostle)	1,480	37
SQUADRON OF CASTILE: MARCOS DE ARAMBURU		
*Galleon San Cristóbal (flagship)	700	26
*Galleon San Felipe y Santiago	530	22
*Galleon San Juan Colorado	530	19
*Galleon Santiago el Mayor	530	17
*Galleon San Medel y Celedon	530	18
*Galleon La Asunción	530	17
*Galleon San Pedro	530	21
SQUADRON OF VIZCAYA: ANTONIO DE URQUIOLA		
Nave Nuestra Señora del Juncal (flagship)	773	26
Nave Santa Maria La Rosa	503	22
Nave Concepción	684	19
Nave Madalena	530	18
Nave Santa Bárbara	525	17
Nave Espíritu Santo	384	20
SQUADRON OF SANCHO PARDO		
*Galleon San Andrés (Apostle — flagship)	1,056	25
Nave Santa Maria La Blanca	720	20
Nave Asunción Gallega		
Nave N.S. de Vegoña de Sevilla	750	16
*Felibote Cavallero de la Mar	190	12
SQUADRON OF PORTUGAL: BARTOLOME VILLAVICENCIO		
*Galleon Santo Tomás (Apostle – flagship)	776	25
*Galleon Santiago de Portugal	520	23
*Galleon San Cristóbal de Portugal	352	21
*Galleon San Bernardo de Portugal	350	17
Nave N.S. de Vegoña de Spinola	900	20
*Felibote Leon Rosso	200	14
SQUADRON OF MARTÍN DE BERTENDONA		
*Galleon San Bernabe (Apostle — flagship)	876	24
Nave N.S. de Vegoña de Landecho	1,001	20
Nave San Juan Baptista de Vizcaya	250	12
Nave El Pilar de Zaragoza	250	16

THE SPANISH FLEET OF 1591

	TONS	GUNS
SQUADRON DE FELIBOTES: LUIS COUTINHO		
La Serena (flagship)		
Leon Bermejo		
Sant Pedro		
Falcon Blanco		
Falcon Pajaro		
Fortuna de Lubeque		
Fortuna de Danzique		
Cazadora (*Caçada*)		
UNATTACHED SHIPS (SUELTOS)		
*Galleon *Caridad Ingles*	200	18
*Navio *San Francisco Inglés* (prize)	190	10
*Navio *San Clemente*	80	8
CARAVELS		
Santiago		
Santiago (not the same ship)		
Anunciada		
Buena Ventura		
San Estevan		
San Antonio		
Nuestra Señora de Ayuda		
PETACHIOS (350 tons in all)		
San Pedro		
San Bernabe		
Nuestra Señora de Puerto		
San Salvador		
La Concepción		
ZABRAS (200 tons in all)		
Nuestra Señora de Gracia		
La Esperanza		
Santa Ana		
Santa Catalina		
Santa Clara		

*Royal ships. Many of the smaller ships also belonged to the King, but these are not distinguished in the list.
Source: AGS GA 341/188 & 204. Felibotes from AGS CM2aE 1234.

finally set sail for Ferrol at the end of June, but even then was delayed by storms for two weeks during which *San Simón*, one of the new galleons, was found to be making so much water that she had to return to port. The great *San Simón* had been planned as Bertendona's flagship, but she was in such poor condition that she had to be left behind and was eventually converted into a merchant carrack. Bertendona now shifted his flag to *San Bernabe*, 'the smallest of them all', and she and the much larger *San Felipe* made their way to Ferrol. These last two Apostles, like those from Santander, were reported to be '*bonissimos*'.[12]

At last, on 17 July, one day after the King's final deadline for departure, the fleet was all ready to sail or rather was nearly all ready since they were still waiting for the arrival of Gaspar de Sousa and his *tercio* of infantry, some Portuguese pilots, 'without whom the armada cannot sail', and a fair wind. Captains, masters and pilots had been chosen for the new galleons from a long list of distinguished applicants eager for such an honourable appointment, men such as Joan de Sancta Maria who had been fighting in the Mediterranean since the 1550s and had served in the relief of Malta in 1565 or Captain Domingo de Yracagan, 'a great sailor' of thirty years' service, 'one of the best seamen in Vizcaya'. Soldiers and sailors had boarded the ships and labourers were loading freshly baked ship's biscuit in sealed casks to protect it from the damp. And, as was customary, alms had been given to the local clergy 'for their work in administering the sacrament to the men of this fleet' and to friars and monks who were to devote themselves to prayers for the *buen sucesso* of the armada.[13]

It was a very impressive fleet, the 'biggest and best that has ever been seen', according to an official in Ferrol. 'Never have so many fine ships been brought together,' wrote Don Alonso de Bazán. There were fifty-nine ships altogether, the fifty-one assembled in Ferrol being reinforced at the last moment by eight armed merchantmen — *felibotes* and *urcas* — which arrived from Lisbon on 19 July under the command of Dom Luis de Coutinho, a distinguished Portuguese soldier. He brought with him five companies of soldiers, some Flemish and Portuguese sailors, large quantities of foodstuffs and wine and fifteen much-needed guns. No fewer than thirty vessels in the fleet were real men-of-war, seventeen galleons and thirteen *naves* from 250 up to 1,500 tons, of which the King owned seventeen and the rest were chartered from private shipowners. The remainder of the fleet consisted of two *felibotes* belonging to the King, two smaller *navios*, seven caravels, five *petachios* and five *zabras*, small and fast ships for reconnaissance, carrying messages among the fleet and maintaining communications with the homeland.[14]

The fleet was organized into seven squadrons with a few ships unattached (see list above). The squadron of the Captain-General had only three ships, but these were all enormous, '*fortissimos* galleons which seemed as towers on the sea' — *San Martín, San Felipe*, the 1,500-ton Apostle from Bilbao, and *San Pablo*, the Apostle flagship in which sailed Don Alonso de Bazán and his staff. The three other Apostles — *San Andrés, Santo Tomás* and *San Bernabe* — became the flagships of the squadrons commanded by Sancho Pardo, Bartolome Villavicencio and '*el valiente*' Martín de Bertendona, the great Basque seaman who was the most experienced of all the squadron commanders. He was about sixty in 1591 and had served the kings of Spain at sea for over forty-five years, first as a boy, then as captain of infantry, captain of ships and commander of squadrons. He had been in the thick of the fighting in the Channel in 1588 and was the only squadron commander in the Armada both to return to Spain in his own ship and still to be alive a few weeks later. In 1589, however, he had been forced to set fire to his own flagship to avoid capture when Drake sailed into Corunna harbour in the *Revenge*. Now, he flew his flag in the fine new *San Bernabe*, with his son Juan proudly beside him, and vowed to have revenge on the *Revenge*.[15]

There were over 7,000 men in the fleet, not counting those on the merchantmen from Portugal. Four thousand of these were soldiers — over 1,000 pikemen and the rest armed with muskets and arquebuses. Nearly all these infantrymen served in the thirty galleons and *naves*, most of which carried at least 100 with the largest contingent being 320 on *San Pablo*, somewhat short of Sir Walter Raleigh's assertion that 'the Spanish ships were filled with companies of souldiers, in some two hundred besides the mariners; in some five, in others eight hundreth.' These men were the main fighting force of Spain at sea, the job of the ships being to get them to battle. The names of many of the captains were proudly reeled off by Andrés Falcão de Resende, a Portuguese poet who in the tradition of Cervantes and

91

Lope de Vega sailed in *San Cristóbal de Portugal*. His epic 'romance' describing the armada of 1591 provides us with much incidental detail and some stirring images. Here it is that we can meet such Spanish and Portuguese heroes as Gaspar de Sousa, a man 'of valour and good council and of heroic spirit', Antonio Leite, 'high in stature and in chivalry', or Tavora d'Anciania, 'brave captain who has grown old at sea'.[16] These were fine men to look at as the hot July sun sparkled on their armour.

There was only one flaw in the praiseworthy achievement of getting such a magnificent fleet to sea less than three years after the heartbreak of 1588. And that was the shortage of guns. Bazán had been adamant that the new galleons at least should be properly armed, 'since they are such majestic ships and capable of carrying good artillery'. He wanted the two largest, *San Pablo* and *San Felipe*, to have no fewer than 50 guns each and the other three between 30 and 40 and ordered the rest of the fleet to be stripped of guns to arm the Apostles. But even this was not enough to bring them up to full strength.[17]

Sir Walter Raleigh was later to describe the guns of the great *San Felipe* as 'three tier of ordinance on a side, and eleven pieces in every tier' — 66 guns not counting those in the bows and stern. In fact, *San Felipe* went to sea with just 37 guns and even the flagship *San Pablo* had only 42. The other three Apostles had only 24 or 25 guns each. Most of the other ships in the fleet were similarly under-gunned. The former flagship *San Martín* had had 48 guns in the Armada campaign and 45 at an earlier muster in 1591, but only 32 when she sailed after being stripped for the sake of the Apostles. *Santiago de Portugal* was reduced from 26 to 23, *San Cristóbal de Portugal* from 26 to 21, and so on. The only squadron which retained or even increased its number of guns were the seven galleons of Castile and these were fairly lightly gunned in any case.[18]

The Spanish fleet was especially deficient in the heavier, ship-battering guns as can be seen in the table opposite. This is based on an undated muster taken sometime before the arrival of Bertendona's squadron and does not include the Apostles or a few other of the galleons and *naves* which were to sail with the fleet. It does, however, include the great majority of the heavy guns, including those which were transferred to the Apostles, since

HEAVY GUNS IN THE SPANISH FLEET

	M/CA	CUL	M/CU	VAR	PED	TOTAL GUNS I	TOTAL GUNS 2
San Martín	2	1	22		8	45	32
San Cristóbal	2		4		4	26	26
San Felipe y Santiago					2	15	22
San Juan Colorado	1	1			4	17	19
Santiago el Mayor					2	15	17
San Medel y Celedon	1				2	16	18
Asunción		1			2	16	17
N.S. del Juncal	2	1		6	2	27	26
Maria La Rosa			3	2	3	23	22
Concepción	1			6	1	28	19
Madalena	1		1	1		24	18
Santa Bárbara			2		2	25	17
Espíritu Santo					4	26	20
Santa Maria la Blanca	5		7		3	18	20
Asunción Gallega	4	1				21	?
Vegoña de Sevilla						5	16
Santiago de Portugal	2		3		7	26	23
Cristóbal de Portugal			6		2	26	21
San Bernardo						6	17
Vegoña de Spinola	3		7		2	27	20

Key: M/Ca =Medio cañón; Cul = Culebrina; M/Cu = Media culebrina;
Var = Varraco; Ped = Pedrero.
Total 1 = Total at earlier muster (see text).
Total 2 = Total at sailing.

WEIGHT OF SHOT IN MAIN SPANISH GUN TYPES
(in Castilian *libras* of 460 grams)

TYPE OF GUN	HIGHEST	LOWEST	AVERAGE	NO. OF GUNS
Medio cañón	24	14	18.2	23
Media culebrina	12	7	9.7	59
Varraco	13	8	10.7	15
Pedrero	29	7	12.1	50
Sacre	7	3.5	5.4	59
Medio sacre	6	2.5	3.7	45
'Piezas de fierro'	9	2.5	3.8	95
Falconete	3	1.5	2.4	95
Esmeril	1	0.5	0.9	23

Source for both tables: AGS GA 341/183. The analysis in
the lower table is confined to the twenty large ships listed above.

it is clear from Bazán's letters that he did not receive many extra guns in the last few weeks, except the fifteen which arrived at the last moment from Lisbon. This muster of artillery must have been very disappointing to the squadron commanders. The twenty galleons and *naves* in the list had only 24 demi-cannon, one single culverin and 59 demi-culverins between them; the only heavy guns with which they were reasonably well equipped were the short-barrelled *pedreros*, some of which threw stone shot and some iron balls. By contrast, the *Revenge* carried 42 guns altogether, of which 2 were demi-cannon and 4 cannon-perriers, all throwing shot of over 20 pounds, no fewer than 10 were culverins firing shot of about 17 or 18 pounds and 8 were demi-culverins.[19] It seems unlikely that the *Defiance*, Lord Thomas Howard's flagship, would have been armed any less strongly than the *Revenge*. Compare these two armaments with those of the ships in the Spanish fleet and it is easy to understand why Don Alonso de Bazán was always worrying about his guns in his letters to the King.

Gunpowder as well as guns was in short supply. The *Revenge* and the *Defiance* both loaded some 90 barrels each containing 100 pounds of gunpowder at the beginning of their voyage, the equivalent of about 90 Spanish quintals. Only one ship in the Spanish fleet had as much as this, *San Pablo*. *San Martín* loaded 64 quintals, seven other ships had 50 quintals and all the rest had less than that, most of them a lot less. Don Juan de Maldonado, the *Veedor-General* or Inspector of the fleet also had serious doubts about the gunners, many of whom had been drafted in from land service and had no experience of naval gunnery. The German gunners received particular scorn, 'men unaccustomed to the sea who arrive encumbered with wives and children who are an embarrassment at sea'. It was perhaps fortunate that Spanish fleets did not normally rely very much on an artillery duel when they went into battle.[20]

Even if it was so short of guns and powder, it was still a fine fleet and it was sad and extremely frustrating that it should have had to endure a series of anti-climaxes before the armada finally sailed out of the land-locked harbour of Ferrol. Time and time again, contrary winds prevented departure and it was not until 4 August that the fleet at last got out, nineteen days after the King's deadline. But this was an auspicious day, the eve of the Assumption of the Virgin Mary, and those waving farewell crossed themselves as they admired the new Apostle galleons who sailed so much faster than the rest of the fleet that they flew past them with the minimum of canvas. But soon sail after sail appeared as the fleet got out to sea and the wind began to hum in the rigging. 'Ease the sheet of the foresail in the name of the Holy Trinity.' Sailors raced to obey the orders of their officers. 'You will see some of them on the topsail yard; others climbing by the ratlines on the shrouds . . . others clinging to the masthead . . . others clambering and chasing from one place to another by the rigging, some high and others low, so that they seem to be cats chasing through the trees.'[21]

By nightfall, the fleet was approaching Cape Finisterre; Don Alonso could proudly address a letter to the King from 'ten leagues out to sea'. Orders were sent to the officers and men in the fleet to do their duty 'for the service of God, the King, and for the common benefit of Christendom'. It was the will of His Majesty that they sail to the island of Flores in the Azores, there to clear the seas of corsairs and escort home the Indies fleets. The *zabras* and *petachios* should sail astern of the flagships of each squadron, 'as near as they can one side and the other', and the men-of-war should follow their flagships in line ahead. Woe to any ship that should leave the line, 'except in case of storm and tempest'.[22]

The Spaniards sailed south and then due west, as the English had done three months before them, and the men of the fleet settled down to the monotonous routine of shipboard life. This differed little from that of the English, save that there was more formal discipline on board a Spanish man-of-war and the soldiers did no work except pike drill and the occasional target practice at white discs set up on the masts. For the rest, it was the usual humdrum pattern of sleep when you could get it, monotonous food, work and more work, gambling and more gambling, and the worship of God. In this last respect, the Spaniards outshone their psalm-singing enemies. Each week, there was a crescendo of prayer, ritual and religious music which reached its climax on Saturday night with the singing of the *Salve Regina*, 'a tempestuous hurricane of music', as Eugenio de Salazar described it. 'If God and his Glorious Mother and the saints to whom we pray looked to our pitch and our voices, and not to our hearts and our spirits, it would do us no good to ask their mercy, with such dissonant howls as we offer them.'[23]

There was, however, little time for the monotony and ritual of the open sea on this voyage. At sunrise on 20 August, just sixteen days out of Ferrol, the rugged cliffs, the hills and green fields of the island of Terceira came into sight and everyone cried: '"Land! Land!", with joy and acclaim.'[24] The campaign of 1591 was about to begin.

PLATE 9 *Corvo seen from the north end of Flores. Site of
the last fight of the* Revenge.

PLATE 10 *The coast of La Serreta in Terceira, probable
wreck-site of the* Revenge.

PLATE 11 *Sir Walter Raleigh, 1588, attributed to the monogrammist 'H'*.

CHAPTER NINE

AT FLORES IN
THE AZORES

At Flores in the Azores
Sir Richard Grenville lay,
And a pinnace,
like a flutter'd bird,
came flying from far away.[1]

T HE NINE RUGGED and beautiful isles of the Azores are little known
to the twentieth-century traveller. Indeed, most people do not even
seem to know where they are. And yet, in the days of sail, the prevailing
wind systems ensured that these Portuguese islands would be of immense
importance as a way station and place of refreshment for ships returning
from such remote places as India, Brazil and the West Indies — 'an hotel
which God had placed in the most convenient spot in the ocean', as a French
consul later described them.[2] The islands lie more or less on the latitude
of Lisbon and are divided into three distinct groups. To the south-east are
Santa Maria and São Miguel, the biggest island which is about 850 miles
from Lisbon. The central group consists of Terceira, the most important
island in our period, São Jorge, Graciosa, Fayal and Pico — aptly named
for its huge peak which often appears to float in the sky while its lower slopes
are enveloped in cloud. Finally, almost equidistant from Portugal and Cape
Race in Newfoundland, lie the most westerly bastions of Europe, the small
island of Flores and the even smaller island of Corvo, so small that it had
no church and had to rely on the services of a priest who only made the
short blustery voyage across from Flores during the season of Lent.[3]

The islands were gradually settled from the middle of the fifteenth
century mainly by people of Portuguese and Flemish origin,[4] but it was in the
sixteenth century that they gained in importance with the rapid expansion

of Portuguese and Spanish oceanic trade. Most ships returning from India or the Americas would call at the islands for fresh water, provisions or to carry out repairs, despite the fact that the Azores were notorious for their storms and did not have one really safe harbour, 'but open bays, subject to all dangers and outerly winds'.[5] Notwithstanding these drawbacks, the islands flourished, merchants grew rich and fine stone houses and churches were built in the main port towns — Villa Franca and Ponta Delgada in São Miguel, Horta in Fayal and Angra, the capital and port of Terceira, the chief city of the islands.

Such prosperity was rudely interrupted in the 1580s, a truly terrible decade for the islanders. All the islands save São Miguel had declared for Dom Antonio and had defied King Philip's claim to the throne of Portugal, a decision which brought about nemesis in the shape of a Spanish fleet commanded by the Marqués of Santa Cruz. In July 1582, he fought and won in the waters of São Miguel the famous 'sea-fight at the islands' against a combined French and Portuguese fleet commanded by Philippe Strozzi. Santa Cruz shocked European opinion by treating his high-born French and Portuguese opponents as pirates, giving orders for them to be executed, despite the pleas of his own officers that 'it did blemish the honour of arms to condemn valiant soldiers to be beheaded and hanged.' But Santa Cruz was adamant. God had determined that the French fleet, sent out in time of peace between France and Spain, should be defeated. The 28 *seigneurs*, 52 knights and 313 soldiers and sailors whom he had taken alive would now pay for this infamous breach of the peace:

> I order . . . the said Lords and gentlemen to be put to death . . . in public, in sight of this fleet and army, on the scaffold built for the purpose in the market square of Villa Franca . . . And the remaining sailors and soldiers . . . who are over seventeen years old, to be hanged, some from the yard-arms of the ships, and others on gallows in the town.[6]

Santa Cruz returned to the Azores in the following summer and, in a brilliant campaign, managed to capture the supposedly impregnable city of Angra in Terceira, after which the other islands fell into Spanish hands.

Once again, this most famous of Spanish sailors demonstrated his ferocity. More of his opponents were executed and Angra was put to the sack for four days, 'firstly by the soldiers, then by the sailors and lastly by the Turks and rabble who came in the galleys', four days which saw the 'greatest sadness, lamentation and horror' in the history of Terceira.[7]

Santa Cruz then departed, leaving the authoritarian Spanish officer Juan de Horbina as governor. He set up a tribunal to overawe those islanders still suspected of loyalty to Dom Antonio and supervised the defences of the islands. Forts were strengthened and multiplied and companies of Spanish and trustworthy Portuguese infantry stationed in the islands, these defences being reinforced after 1588. However, as elsewhere in the Spanish Empire, there was not enough money or men to defend the islands completely, even though the lack of landing places and surrounding cliffs made them comparatively easy to defend. Only Terceira, São Miguel and, to a lesser extent, Fayal, were well fortified; there were a few guns and soldiers on Graciosa and Santa Maria, but the other islands were largely left to protect themselves and were supplied with virtually no weapons. Just one hundred soldiers would be enough to protect the landing places of remote Flores and Corvo, pleaded Juan de Horbina in a letter to the King. But such an appeal, like countless others by colonial governors, fell on deaf ears and these little islands lay 'open to all the world and to whosoever will come thither, as well Englishmen as others, for that the inhabitants have not the power to resist them'.[8]

A few English ships sailed with the fleet defeated by Santa Cruz in 1582 but not many, as the Queen was not yet committed to war with Spain. A great chance was thus lost. Had England supported Dom Antonio with more strength and so maintained his control of the islands, the war against Spanish trade would have been very much more effective. No longer would the Spanish Indies fleets have been able to shelter and restore themselves in the Azores. No longer would the treasure from the fleets have been unloaded and stored in the castle of Angra to protect it from the English or from a sinking ship, a sight which was to amaze the Dutch merchant Linschoten in November 1589 when 'the whole quay lay covered with plates and chests of silver full of ryales of eight, most wonderful to behold . . . besides pearles, gold and other stones.'9 Instead, Terceira and the other islands would have become an English bastion athwart the routes of the treasure fleets. But England did not fight in 1582 and this was not to be.

As it was, the islands were to swarm with English corsairs every year, once war with Spain became a reality in 1585. But these corsairs did little to make themselves loved by the islanders, people whose loyalty to Spain was ambivalent to say the least and who might have been useful allies. We have seen how Sir Richard Grenville ravished the Azores in 1586 and so became 'greatlie feared in these Islands and knowne of every man'. His example was soon followed. In the summer of 1587, men from five English corsair ships landed at Lajes, the second town of Flores. The inhabitants fled safely into the woods, but the town was sacked. The corsairs then marched on and burned down Santa Cruz, the capital of the island which two years later was still 'all ruinous, and (as it were) but the reliques of the ancient towne'. In this year, 1589, it was the turn of Horta in Fayal which was raided by the Earl of Cumberland. The castle was captured, the batteries dismounted and forty-five guns taken into the Earl's ships. Then, despite his stern prohibition on plunder, some of his men 'sacked and spoiled the town, and after ransomed it'. Cumberland did manage to save the churches and convents from the looters, by placing a guard on them, and it was in fact chiefly in church plate that the town's ransom was paid. The English then invited the chief people of Horta to dinner on board the *Victory* and, as they departed after their meal, saluted them 'with sound of drum and a peal of ordnance'.10 Horta was soon refortified by the Spaniards, but the vulnerability of all the islands except Terceira had been clearly demonstrated. Meanwhile, the English had made few friends despite their dinner invitations and chivalrous salutes. Indeed, the normal reaction of the islanders to the appearance of corsairs was to grab everything of value and disappear into the interior, driving their animals before them. When asked 'what was the cause thereof, they answered, feare'.11

It was then with some apprehension that the people of the Azores heard that yet another English fleet was on its way towards them and that Don Ricardo de Campoverde was its vice-admiral. What that fleet had been doing since 9 May when they captured the advice boat from

Havana is something of a mystery. No letters or dispatches from either Grenville or Lord Thomas Howard have survived and there is only one letter from Philip Gawdy in the *Revenge* which is dated 6 June. By this time, the galleon was in the Azores and Philip told his brother that 'we staye and pray every day hartely for the Spanishe fleetes coming, and if they come not sodeynly [i.e. soon] I thank God we are and shall be sufficiently provided to look for their longer coming.' Philip as usual was very cheerful — 'I never had my health better in my lyfe' — and was enjoying such wonders of the sea as dolphins and flying fish. But he has nothing to say about what the fleet was actually doing in the Azores, save that 'we watered at flowers' by which he means the island of Flores.[12]

What was happening on a day-by-day basis will probably never be known, but there is sufficient evidence to piece together the general outline of the activities of Lord Thomas and Sir Richard Grenville. One report tells us, for instance, that 'English ships covered the seas of Azores and that they had saccaged [sacked] São Miguel.' This was an island well known to English sailors, particularly those from west-country ports, who sailed there to exchange English cloth for the woad grown in the islands. This traffic was banned after war broke out, but to no effect since the English continued to trade 'under the names of Scots and French men', one sign among many of the inability of the Spaniards to control the islands. Such sailors and merchants were useful sources of local information and corsairs were advised to make contact with them, 'and to avoid suspicion and danger . . . you shall speak with them in the night.' No doubt the men of Lord Thomas's fleet did this and no doubt they also looked into the roadstead of Angra in Terceira, 'to see in what state the ships there ride' — an elementary intelligence operation performed by virtually all corsairs in the islands.[13]

Meanwhile, the expedition was not totally devoid of profit as can be seen from the prize records kept by the investors in England. On 10 June, a small caravel laden with molasses and sugar was taken and, nearly seven weeks later, a ship laden with sugar from São Tome. This was slow work and it is clear that the word had gone out far and wide that English corsairs were loose in the Azores so that most ships avoided the islands, though on 11 August a big vessel from Brazil with 600 chests of sugar was taken. These prizes were sent home to the investors. Meanwhile, letters from England arrived in the Azores, most often carried by the busy and fast-sailing Captain Fleming in the *Dolphin* of Plymouth, but there was still no sign of the treasure ships.[14]

Some of the privateers attached to the English fleet sailed hundreds of miles out into the Atlantic as an advance watch. However, the main body of Howard's fleet patrolled 'sixty leagues west of Fayal, spreading north and south betwixt 37½ and 38½ degrees'. This area, to the south-west of Flores, was the rendezvous which had been given to the armed merchantmen from London, though these valuable reinforcements did not arrive until the end of the first week of September, too late to join up with the royal fleet. Other English ships were cruising further to the north, in the waters between Flores and Corvo, where 'the Englishmen doe commonly stay, to watch the ships that come out of the West'. While they did so, they found time to pillage these defenceless islands. On 15 July, Gaspar Pimentel, captain of the island of Flores, managed to smuggle out a letter to Juan de Horbina in Terceira. He reported that corsairs under the command of Sir Richard Grenville had landed on his island 'and burned the churches and many houses in the villages . . . They stole many sheep and pigs.' The churches in Fayal may have been saved from the Protestant wrath of the men of the Earl of Cumberland, but Flores got no such protection and this in an island singled out from all others for its 'faith, piety and devotion'.[15]

If it seemed to the people of Flores that God had forgotten them, their experience was nothing to that of São Miguel. In July 1591, the island was struck by a devastating earthquake. The town of Villa Franca was destroyed and 'the ships which lay in the roads and on the sea shaked as if the world would have turned round . . . They heard such thunder and noise under the earth as if all the devils in Hell had been assembled in that place, wherewith many dyed for fear.'[16] Whether the English ships were shaken in the waters of the western islands and their sailors heard the voice of doom is not known. But as July turned into August there were fewer signs of the former high spirits. The fleet had been at sea now for over four months and was becoming very short of provisions, despite the fresh supplies convoyed out by the *Golden Lion* and the *Foresight*. Refugees from Corvo reported that the English had little to eat and had cut their rations.[17]

For such robbers to go hungry in the Azores was ironic, since the islands were a cornucopia of food and drink. Linschoten drools over the varieties of foodstuffs available in Terceira, giving particular emphasis to 'a certaine fruite that groweth under the earth . . . it beareth a fruite called Batatas [i.e. potato] that is very good . . . but little esteemed and yet it is a great sustenance and foode for the common sorte of people.' Flores, with its stony soil, was not as fertile as Terceira, but it was 'full of cattle and other necessarie provisions', while Corvo was '*fertilissima*', a storehouse of 'excellent fruits of the sea, the air and of the land'. How could the islanders have managed to keep all this provender safe from the ravenous attention of the English?[18]

Perhaps there were just too many Englishmen — not far short of 2,000 in all, only a little less than the total population of the two western islands. Or perhaps the English were too sick to search the wild landscape for the sheep and goats and cattle and pigs, for the corn and vegetables and wine concealed there. For sickness, as so often in the Elizabethan navy, had struck the fleet. As early as 23 July, Howard had been forced to send home one of the Queen's galleons, the 500-ton *Nonpareil*, on account of 'the great infection of the ship', and some of the privateers had followed in her wake. As the weeks of August passed, infection spread through the rest of the fleet. By the last week of the month, 'the one halfe part of the men of every shippe' were sick 'and utterly unserviceable'. Worst hit of all was the *Bonaventure* which had sailed from England with 250 men, but now had 'not so many in health as could handle her maine saile'. Disease had also struck the crew of the *Revenge*, ninety of whom were sick by the end of August, according to Sir Walter Raleigh.[19] What form the sickness took is unknown, but it was probably a combination of scurvy and of enteric diseases brought on by rotten food and foul beer and water. Such diseases spread quickly in the close and insanitary constraint of an Elizabethan galleon.

Lord Thomas Howard was thus faced with many problems. His stores were very low, his men sick and his ships foul after so many months at sea. The season was advancing and there was growing danger of storms which often struck the islands in August and particularly in September. And there was still no sign of the treasure fleets. Could they possibly have passed him by? Howard needed to decide what course to follow. The orders from England which he had received in the Azores left him with considerable discretion: 'You are well to consider, upon such good intelligence as you shall get, whether it be better for you to attend about the islands to meet with the Indian fleet, or to come to the south cape of Spain and there to abide their coming home.' It was up to Lord Thomas, though the advice from England suggested that the latter course might be the better one.

Howard had thought otherwise and had stayed in the Azores. However, now that he had spent so long 'attending' fruitlessly about the islands, he decided it was time to follow the second course of cruising off the coast of Spain. Indeed, it seems probable that he had always planned to leave for Spain at the end of August, judging from his instructions to Captain Robert Flicke, the commander of the ships fitted out by the City of London. Flicke had been told to meet Howard at the rendezvous south-west of Flores up to the end of August but, after that, to meet him off Cape Roca on the coast of Portugal.[20]

Howard's fleet at this point consisted of the four powerful galleons of the Queen — *Defiance, Revenge, Bonaventure* and *Golden Lion* — and two smaller Queen's ships, *Foresight* and *Crane*, together with privateers, pinnaces and victuallers whose numbers are not certain. The 250-ton privateer *Galleon Raleigh* was certainly there, as were the 120-ton *Pilgrim* and 100-ton *Lyons Whelp*. But we cannot be sure about the numbers and identity of the other smaller ships, though probably most of those in the second list on page 53 were still with the fleet — a total of between fourteen and twenty-two ships depending on whether one believes the English or Spanish sources.[21]

Whatever the exact numbers, much had to be done before the fleet could sail for the coast of Portugal. Lord Thomas had a good reputation for looking after his men — 'for the good usage of all his followers of all sorts and degrees, but speciallie for the poor toiling and continual labouring mariners' — and care of the sick was his first priority. He brought his fleet to anchor off Flores and had the sick men taken ashore to enjoy fresh food and water and to recover in the more wholesome air of the island. He then set about the watering and cleansing, or 'rummaging', of his ships. The gravel ballast from London river, now unbelievably foul from bilge, human waste and the dregs of food and drink, was thrown overboard and replaced with clean stones. Meanwhile, the interiors of the ships were scrubbed and fumigated with vinegar and the casks cleaned ready to receive fresh water from the island. This was necessary work, but it had to be done quickly, since his ships would be very vulnerable while they were being cleansed. No commander likes to have half his men ashore and his ships so light that they would be unable to carry full sail in an emergency.[22]

The sources do not state exactly where Lord Thomas Howard was anchored in these last days of August 1591. However, it seems clear from the evidence available that he must have been in the normal *ancoradouro* or anchorage of Flores. This was in the north-east of the island, just south of the small village of Ponta Delgada, where there was good water available. On 28 August, the wind moved into the east and Lord Thomas no doubt shifted into the lee of Ponta Ruiva, which juts out on the south-east side of the anchorage, so as to prevent his ships from being caught on a lee shore. Meanwhile, he would have kept a pinnace or two out at sea on the west side of the island to look out for the expected Indies fleet. One Spanish source says that he also had men in *atalayas* or watch-towers high up on the west coast of the island. The English evidence says nothing about this, but it would have been a sensible thing to do.[23]

No one appears to have thought it necessary to have look-outs or advice boats to provide notice of dangers from the east or south-east. Letters from England had stressed that Spain's greatest armed strength — twenty-two or twenty-three warships — would be actually sailing from Havana with the treasure fleets and had mentioned, only as an afterthought, 'some intelligence . . . of certayne shippes that the Kinge of Spayne dothe send to the Islandes'. No letter from England mentioned the information provided as long ago as 3 December 1590 by the 'well-willer of Her Majesty' in Andalucia 'that in August the army at Ferrol would go to the Azores'. The correspondent had warned the English that 'a good army' would be needed in the islands 'or else the Spaniards would prevail'.[24] Lord Thomas Howard and Sir Richard Grenville knew nothing of that.

It was not until the early morning of 30 August that they at last got warning of the danger that threatened them from the east. This was when 'a pinnace, like a flutter'd bird, came flying from far away', as Tennyson described her. She was the delightfully named *Moonshine*, a small privateer ship from London commanded by Captain William Myddelton. He had been serving in the Bay of Biscay with Cumberland's fleet when the Earl discovered that Bazán's armada had sailed from Ferrol and was headed for the Azores. Cumberland was then on the point of returning to England after his disappointing summer, but he could hardly keep such news to himself and so dispatched the *Moonshine*, the fastest ship in his fleet, to warn Lord Thomas and Sir Richard Grenville of the danger sailing towards them. Myddelton caught up with the Spanish fleet in the Azores and sailed in their company for three days to discover their intentions, before heading for Flores only a few hours ahead of Bazán and his armada. No doubt his report to Lord Thomas was framed in good nautical prose, but Tennyson has admirably captured the menace of his message: 'Spanish ships of war at sea! We have sighted fifty-three!'[25]

CHAPTER TEN

FIVE IN THE AFTERNOON

Lo demás era muerte y solo muerte
a los cinco de la tarde.

The rest was death and death alone
at five in the afternoon.[1]

W HEN DON ALONSO DE BAZÁN came to anchor at Angra on 20 August,
he could feel pleased with the performance of his fleet after the long
delays in Spain. The only serious problem had been the Apostle *Santo Tomás*
which had been so badly rigged in Santander that she nearly lost all three of
her masts. Otherwise, the voyage had gone well. Sixteen days from Ferrol to
Terceira was not bad going and Don Alonso was now eager to lead his fleet
into action against the English. On arrival in Terceira, he asked the governor,
Juan de Horbina, what news he had of the strength of the English fleet at
Flores. Horbina had received a number of conflicting reports, but thought
there might be as many as forty ships around the western islands.[2]

Don Alonso sent a pinnace back to Spain with the news of his arrival
and then ordered his squadron commanders to set sail at once in search
of the English, though one suspects that the 'at once' was for the benefit of
the King rather than the truth, since the fleet was still making purchases
of meat and other supplies in Terceira three days after its arrival in the
island.[3] In any event, progress was very slow as contrary winds and flat
calms delayed their passage to the north-west. Day after day, the fleet beat
to windward and not until 28 August, eight days after arriving in Terceira,
did they manage to cover the forty or fifty miles to the channel between the
islands of Graciosa and São Jorge.

During this period of frustration, Don Alonso received more accurate
information about the strength of the enemy fleet. This came from a
Franciscan friar and a ship's pilot who had spent several days as prisoners

107

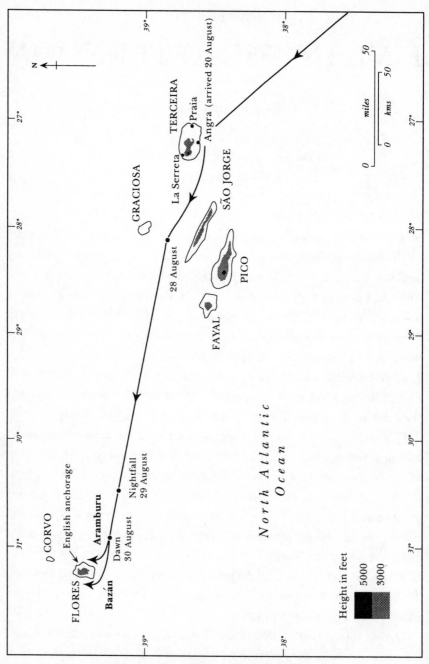

N

CORVO

FLORES
English anchorage
Aramburu
Bazán
Dawn
30 August
Nightfall
29 August

31°

30°

29°

28°

27°

39°

GRACIOSA

La Serreta   TERCEIRA
Praia
Angra (arrived 20 August)

28 August

SÃO JORGE

PICO

FAYAL

North Atlantic
Ocean

Height in feet

5000

3000

miles   50
0
kms   50
0   27°

39°

38°

28°

29°

30°

31°

38°

DIAGRAM 2 *Map of the route of the Spanish fleet to the
western islands.*

on Lord Thomas Howard's *Defiance*. They stated that there were no more than twenty-two ships, including six large galleons of the Queen. There were in fact only five large galleons, if one counts the 360-ton *Foresight* as large, but Don Alonso's informants had probably included the 250-ton private ship *Galleon Raleigh* in their total.

Bazán must have been relieved to learn that the English fleet was so much weaker than his own. His satisfaction increased in the early afternoon of 28 August when the wind changed into the east and so promised him a speedy passage for the remaining 150 miles to the western islands. The fleet clapped on as much sail as possible and, by nightfall on the following day — the Feast of the Nativity of the Virgin — the pilots reported that they were now only fifty miles from Flores and in the same latitude.

Don Alonso now did what every Spanish commander did when battle, and possible disaster, loomed close. He called a *junta* of his squadron commanders to determine what action they should take. It was always wise for those in command in the Spanish Empire to record on paper a well-reasoned, joint decision. However, on this occasion, there can have been little doubt as to the correct course of action. A weaker English fleet was just fifty miles to leeward and there was no time to be lost. It was resolved to sail on through the night, 'since the wind was fresh and favourable to our purpose', and to come upon the unsuspecting enemy in his anchorage at daybreak.

This bold plan was thwarted by another mishap to one of the Apostles, this time *San Andrés*, the flagship of the squadron commanded by Sancho Pardo. He sent word to Don Alonso that his bowsprit had broken and he was no longer able to carry a full suit of sails.[4] Rather than leave this one galleon to fall behind, Don Alonso sent his *zabras* round the fleet to order every ship to shorten sail so as to keep *San Andrés* company. This order was given for fear the galleon might be attacked when on her own, no doubt a noble motive, but the decision ensured that Bazán would lose the total surprise which until then had been possible. No longer under full sail, the fleet made only moderate progress through the rest of the night and, as dawn broke, was still about twenty-seven miles from Flores, whose hills could be discerned from the mastheads as the sun rose in the sky. The wind still blew strongly from the east, but the English had been given a few hours' grace.

Soon after this same dawn of 30 August, Captain Myddelton in the *Moonshine* arrived at Howard's anchorage to warn him of Bazán's approach. This was devastating news. Here was the English fleet at anchor, with half its men on shore and many of the ships still without their ballast, and an armada of fifty-three ships only hours away. There was not a minute to lose. Further cleansing of the ships was abandoned and all fit men assigned to reballast the empty vessels. Hour after hour the work went on as boats shuttled to and from the shore, loaded to the gunwales with baskets full of stones. This work was an absolute priority, since without ballast the galleons would be unable to carry their full suit of canvas for fear of capsizing. Back and forth went the boats, while the look-outs at the mastheads and on the point kept an anxious eye out to sea for the approach of the Spanish fleet.

Before the English could even start this work, Don Alonso was once again on the move. He sent a *zabra* forward to reconnoitre the enemy's position and then divided his fleet 'so as to put the enemy . . . between two fires'. This was a subtle ruse. General Marcos de Aramburu would approach the English from the south-east and head for the straits between Flores and Corvo with the seven galleons of Castile, or of Seville as they were often called, together with four smaller vessels — eleven ships in all. Don Alonso with the other forty-odd ships would sail towards the south of Flores in order to round the island and so surprise the English fleet by coming at them from the south-west, the direction from which they were expecting the treasure fleets. The squadron of flyboats under Dom Luis Coutinho took the starboard station, next to the three huge galleons of the Captain-General. Further to port were the squadrons of Bertendona, Sancho Pardo and Urquiola, while the squadron of Portugal under Bartolome Villavicencio brought up the rear.

The approach of the two Spanish fleets presented an amazing sight to the people of Flores — farmers, fishermen and shepherds — as they lined the cliffs in the east and south-east of their island and marvelled at the gret galleons of Spain, painted sails billowing and flags and streamers out before them in the fresh east wind. These people had once been friends to the English who had often watered in their island and paid fair money for the victuals that they needed. But they no longer wished the English well and did not warn them of what they could see before their eyes. Don Ricardo de Campoverde, that 'great heretic and persecutor of Catholics', had stolen their livestock and burned their churches to the ground. As they stared at the armada of Spain, they could only hope that the English, and especially Don Ricardo in the *Revenge*, would reap the fate they so richly deserved.

By noon, the main Spanish force had reached the south-east of the island.[5] But now fortune favoured the English, giving them precious moments of time to complete ballasting the ships and get the sick men aboard. The cause of this good fortune was Dom Luis Coutinho and his lumbering flyboats on the right of Don Alonso's fleet. As they sailed round the south of the island, Coutinho's squadron which was nearest to the shore became becalmed in the lee of a headland. Once again, the other ships were ordered to shorten sail and wait until Coutinho had extracted himself and other stragglers in the fleet had caught up. Once Don Alonso had a plan, he liked to carry it out to the letter, even at the cost of vital time.

The main body of the fleet now rounded the south-west point of Flores and sailed up the west coast of the island, with the wind on their starboard beam. Meanwhile, the squadron of Castile led by Marcos de Aramburu in *San Cristóbal* took the shorter route up the east coast of the island, no doubt shortening sail so as not to arrive too soon at the English anchorage in the north-east of the island. They were separated from the English by high and very rugged country, with several hills of over 1,000 feet, and there was no danger that their approach would be observed by the English look-outs. Hearts beat a little faster as the two Spanish fleets approached nearer to the enemy. 'Get ready, friends . . . And then, in every ship, the soldiers and sailors with a loud voice cried, "To arms! To arms!"' wrote the armada's excited poet, Falcão de Resende.[6]

These last moments before the fight were very busy as the ships and men were put in readiness. Guns were loaded and muskets and arquebuses inspected one more time. Swords and daggers were sharpened by the carpenter and his mates. Baskets of stones were brought up from the ballast, some to be hoisted to the fighting tops, others taken to the forecastle and sterncastle where ample store of other missiles, such as grenades, fire arrows and darts were also stacked ready for action. Pikes, javelins and lances were placed along the decks ready to be snatched up to repel boarders. Mattresses were set up as protection against enemy fire and missiles. Barrels of vinegar were prepared for cleaning the guns and water tubs were placed everywhere to protect the ship against the very likely risk of fire, a reservoir being provided by one of the ship's boats filled with water. Meanwhile, the soldiers adjusted their helmets, buckled on their breastplates and picked up their shields and weapons before moving to their fighting positions.[7]

By mid-afternoon, the main body of the Spanish fleet, approaching the north end of the island, was at last seen by the English pinnace stationed in the straits between Flores and Corvo. Day after day, week after week, men had stood in the tops scanning the seas to the west and south-west for an incoming fleet. Now at last one had come. The pinnace hastened to Lord Thomas's anchorage, firing off her guns and striking her topsails as a sign that she had sighted the enemy. As she came up to the *Defiance*, her captain cried out that they had seen the treasure fleets coming from the south-west. Don Alonso's ruse had worked.

By this time, the English had almost completed the arduous work which had occupied them all day and were ferrying aboard the last of the sick men from the shore. The exciting news of the treasure fleets put out of their minds all thought of an armada from the east. Look-outs had scanned the eastern horizon all day and had seen nothing, so there seemed to be no danger. And now the treasure fleets were at hand. As long ago as May Day, Philip Gawdy had written that the men of the *Revenge* were 'like lions that have been almost famished for want of prey'.[8] How hungry for prizes they must have been by 30 August!

Lord Thomas Howard ordered his fleet to get under way at once to intercept the treasure fleets. The crews dashed to the orders of masters and pilots, some being in such a hurry that they cut their cables and left their anchors behind. Since action was imminent, the galleons of the Queen set only their fighting sails — topsails and main foresail. Their huge mainsails were left furled on the yards, since they would have made the ships heel over in the breeze and so prevent the guns on the lee side from being used.

Lord Thomas led the fleet out of the anchorage, the other ships sailing in line behind him. Two tacks were probably needed to weather the most northerly point of Flores before turning to the west to bar the passage of the fleets from the Indies. With the wind behind him, he could now dictate the course of the approaching battle.

The last ship to leave her berth and so the last in the English line by a long way was the *Revenge*. Why should Sir Richard Grenville have been so slow off the mark? There has been much speculation on this point.[9] Was it because his ship had still not finished taking on its fresh ballast? Was it because the *Revenge* was anchored closer inshore than the rest of the fleet and had difficulty getting under way with an east wind blowing? Was it simply arrogance based on a belief that the *Revenge* was so fast that she could catch up the rest of the fleet at leisure? Or was it because of Grenville's care for his men, as Sir Walter Raleigh claimed? 'Sir Richard Grenville was the last that weighed, to recover the men that were upon the island.' A noble cause that Tennyson embroiders delightfully:

> Sir Richard bore in hand all his sick men from the land
> Very carefully and slow,
> Men of Bideford in Devon,
> And we laid them on the ballast down below.

Taking the sick men aboard was certainly honourable and would have delayed Grenville, but presumably no more than other ships some of which, such as the *Bonaventure*, had far more sick men ashore than the *Revenge*. Sir Richard's slow departure remains a mystery. He may have been last simply because his ship was the vice-admiral whose normal position was at the rear of the line, but this would not explain the big gap in the line. Whatever the reason, Grenville was hardly out of the anchorage as the leading English ships were weathering the point at the extreme north of Flores, three-quarters of a league behind according to one Spanish account.[10]

As the first English ships rounded the point, a pinnace scouting out in front of Don Alonso's armada signalled that she had sighted the enemy by raising and lowering her main topsail four times and by firing two shots.

Her guns were echoed almost immediately by two shots from the east fired by Marcos de Aramburu in *San Cristóbal*, the flagship of the squadron of Castile. He had timed his approach to perfection. His route up the east coast had been shrouded completely from the English by the configuration of the coastline and by the high land to the south-east of the English anchorage. Bazán and Aramburu were now on course to catch the enemy 'between two fires' as planned. Don Alonso might have been a cautious man, but his caution here ensured that an extremely difficult naval manoeuvre was carried out almost without flaw. Two fleets, separated by some ten miles of very hilly island, had arrived at the same place at almost exactly the same time.

The moment that Lord Thomas Howard saw the leading ships of the Spanish fleet, the extreme danger of his position became apparent. He may have been 'a mere youngster and no sailor', but he had served with distinction against the Armada and would therefore have known at once that the approaching Spanish ships were no treasure fleet. Indeed, he later described what he saw as 'the greatest and finest armada that he had ever seen'.[11] In the van were the three leviathans of the squadron of the Captain-General, including *San Martín* — Medina Sidonia's flagship in 1588 — which half the men on the *Defiance* would have recognized. Worse still, Howard could also see to starboard the leading ships of the squadron of Castile on a course to get to windward of him and so prevent him escaping from the main Spanish battle fleet. In such circumstances, discretion was certainly the correct course for the commander of a fleet so heavily outnumbered. Lord Thomas Howard, as Tennyson assures us, was no coward, but he needed to change course and do so quickly to escape from the jaws of the trap set by Don Alonso. He ordered 'his fleet not to fall upon' the Spaniards, but to set their mainsails and bear up to the north.[12]

This course carried him across the front of the squadron of Castile in the direction of the island of Corvo. The leading ships in both the Spanish fleets clapped on even more sail and, with trumpets sounding and men cheering to the beat of the drum, tried desperately to close the gap through which Lord Thomas threatened to elude them. The gunners loosed their tackles, knocked out their ports and rolled out their guns. A

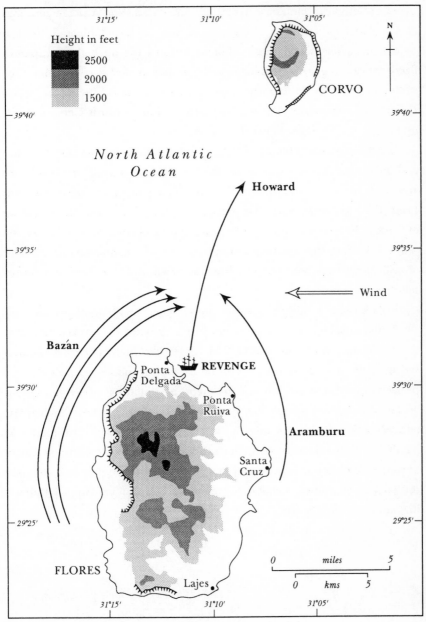

DIAGRAM 3 *Map of events at five in the afternoon,*
30 August 1591.

banner of crimson damask was hoisted in *San Pablo* and a single gun fired as the signal for battle to commence. At five in the afternoon,[13] the gap narrowed sufficiently for Lord Thomas to open fire on both the Spanish fleets whose vanguards exchanged artillery and musket fire with him. One well-aimed shot by an English gunner seriously damaged the rigging of *San Cristóbal* and then Lord Thomas was away, sailing towards Corvo and out of danger, the Spanish ships left safely behind.

The disappointed Spaniards hurled abuse and demanded that he stand and fight, but to no avail. Don Martín de Bertendona later said that Howard's ships fled, 'as if they had the devil himself at their heels', but Lord Thomas would not have seen it like that. Once past the squadron of Castile, he bore up closer to the wind and headed north-east to take the weather station, the position desired by all naval commanders in the days of sail. Here, with both Spanish fleets to leeward of him, he could run or fight as he chose.[14]

It had been a fairly close-run thing. Such small accidents can lay the foundations of success or failure; in this case, the broken bowsprit on *San Andrés* which had caused Don Alonso to order his fleet to shorten sail in their passage towards Flores. If he had abandoned *San Andrés* and pressed on with full sail through the night, he would have been in position at dawn to capture or sink the whole of the English fleet as it lay helpless at anchor. He did not do this and so 'let a great victory slip through his hands', as the contemporary Spanish historian Cabrera de Córdoba was to lament in his fine description of the battle.[15] But Don Alonso still had the chance of a lesser victory, for one ship had not yet slipped through his hands — the *Revenge*.

CHAPTER ELEVEN

FOR THE REST OF THE DAY

Shall we fight or shall we fly?
Good Sir Richard, tell us now,
For to fight is but to die![1]

T HE SIGHT THAT greeted Sir Richard Grenville, as he belatedly rounded the north point of Flores, would have amazed a battle-hardened sailor, let alone a man who had never before seen an enemy fleet. We do not know for certain how far he was behind the main body of the English fleet. A Spanish account says that he was three-quarters of a league behind, or about two and a quarter English nautical miles, but this may be a slight exaggeration since at least one and probably three of the smaller English ships were still in company with the *Revenge*.[2] But, however far behind he was, it was too far for comfort; for now there was no gap between the two Spanish fleets for Sir Richard to sail through and so join Lord Thomas Howard.

The sun was beginning to go down in the west as he stood on the poop of the *Revenge* and surveyed the deep blue sea of the straits between Flores and Corvo. It was covered with Spanish ships. To his left were the cliffs of the north coast of Flores and then, filling the western middle distance, were the forty-two or more ships of Don Alonso's fleet headed by the three mighty galleons of his own squadron. Further to the right, with no discernible break in the line, were the eleven ships of Marcos de Aramburu led by the seven galleons of the squadron of Castile. Beyond them and beyond reach, sailing close-hauled to the north-east, were the *Defiance* and the other English ships with Lord Thomas Howard and, beyond them, like a beached whale on the horizon, was the little island of Corvo, its high point haloed in cloud.

Sir Richard Grenville had two courses open to him — the course of honour and the course of discretion. Now that he was cut off from his

117

friends by such a massively powerful fleet, it would have been politic to have turned tail and run. There were no formal rules of engagement but, a few years earlier, Grenville's predicament had been covered by William Blandy in his description of a 'fortunate commander'. Such a man was one who knew when to run as well as fight; 'in perill to escape, in place to pursue, in necessity to stand fast, in doubt to be quickly and prudently resolved'.[3] Sir Richard was certainly 'in perill', but there was still room to escape by sailing due west between the rearguard of Don Alonso's fleet and the coast of Flores. This was the course urged by his master who was certainly no coward. As the *Revenge* was still wearing her fighting sails, the master commanded that the rope holding her great mainsail in place on the yard be cut 'that they might make away'. Sir Richard's reaction to this order was terrifying to behold. He rounded on the master in fury and 'threatened both him, and all the rest that were in the ship, that if any man laid hand upon it, he would cause him to be hanged'.[4] The crew stood back abashed and left the mainsail furled.

The course of discretion was simply impossible for a gentleman as proud as Sir Richard Grenville, a man who did not have it in his nature to be prudent. Rather than run, as Sir Walter Raleigh put it, 'he would rather choose to die, than to dishonour himself, his country and Her Majesty's ship.' But did he fully realize what he was doing as he so furiously countermanded his master's order? Spanish accounts suggest that, at this point, Grenville still did not appreciate that what he saw ahead of him was the armada of Spain and not the treasure fleets. This seems unlikely. Sir Richard, unlike Lord Thomas, had never before seen a Spanish armada and so might possibly not know one when he saw it. However, this was not true of many of the men under his command who could easily identify for him such famous ships as *San Martín* and *San Cristóbal*.

No, Sir Richard certainly knew what lay ahead when he ignored the master's advice, but the knowledge did not deter him. He ordered the *Revenge* to clear for action; her guns were run out, her painted waistcloths rigged to conceal the men on deck from the enemy's musketeers, her flags, streamers and pennants hoisted. As the men ran to carry out these tasks, the helmsman was ordered to steer directly for the squadron of Castile which

Grenville hoped to break through and so take up his correct position in the rear of Lord Thomas Howard's fleet. Consequently, to the amazement of the Spaniards, the *Revenge* sailed straight towards them — 'valueing the world as nothing', as Bertendona put it; 'advancing towards our fleet with *arrogancia*' in the words of the Portuguese poet. Sir Richard had chosen his course, though even his admiring kinsman Sir Walter Raleigh thought that 'the other course had been better'.[5]

Did the men of the *Revenge* cheer at the boldness of their commander's decision? Or did they sing a psalm, like the crew of the *Content*, as they sailed closer to the Spanish fleet? We do not know. We do not even know for sure how many men there were aboard the *Revenge* as she went into action. Sir Walter Raleigh claimed there were only 190, of whom ninety were sick and 'laid in hold upon the ballast', the safest place in a battle. But Sir Walter was at pains to emphasize the odds against the English and his figures are almost certainly wrong. The official Spanish *relación* said there were 250 men on the English galleon and this is likely to be nearer the correct number. The *Revenge* sailed from Plymouth with a crew of 260, some of whom were sent home with the prizes, but were in turn replaced by foreigners from the prizes taken, as happened when the *Eagle* of Lubeck was captured. A few men may have died in the Azores, but not many, since it is sickness and not death that is emphasized in accounts of the infection that struck the English fleet. So there were probably about 250 men on the *Revenge*, some of whom, perhaps as many as ninety, were lying 'on the ballast down below', leaving 160 men to shout the battlecries of England as they approached the Spanish fleet — 'God save the captain and the company' and 'Saint George for England.'[6]

Sir Richard ordered the helmsman to steer towards the leading galleons of the squadron of Castile on his weather bow. As they closed, the English opened fire with their great guns and then at the last moment the *Revenge* suddenly altered course closer to the wind and, 'as the mariners terme it, sprang their luff'.[7] This move took the *Revenge* to windward of the leading galleons and forced them under her lee. It was a bold move, worthy of the man whom the Spaniards called a 'great sailor', and it appeared to have been successful. Now there was a gap among the galleons of Castile and the way lay open for the *Revenge* to sail through it close-hauled and catch up Lord

Thomas Howard, anxiously watching his vice-admiral's daring attempt to rejoin the English fleet.

The Spaniards set off in pursuit, led by Don Alonso with the three great galleons of his squadron and Martín de Bertendona in his flagship, the Apostle *San Bernabe*. The clumsy *San Martín* soon fell behind and then Don Alonso's flagship, *San Pablo*, faltered. Her masthead had been damaged earlier in the day and she could no longer carry her main topsail — yet another Apostle to disappoint King Philip on her maiden voyage. Four out of six of these fine new ships had been found wanting, clear evidence of over-hasty and shoddy work by the riggers in the shipyards. But the other two — *San Felipe* and *San Bernabe* — would prove the competence of their designers and builders. These were the largest and the smallest of the Apostles built in the yards at Bilbao. From the moment of their trials in the waters of Biscay, their strength and speed had impressed all those who saw them. The *San Felipe* was not, as the historian Sir Geoffrey Callender described her, 'an unwieldy carrack'. She was very big, but she was still a galleon built 'on English lines'. Nor was she 'a slug compared with the *Revenge*', as the *Revenge* was now to discover when the huge *San Felipe* began to overhaul her.[8]

San Felipe carried the very finest infantry in the Spanish fleet, 223 soldiers in all, including the hand-picked volunteers in the company of Don Francisco de Toledo and a number of high-spirited gentlemen adventurers from Lisbon.[9] These were men to whom storming a fortress or boarding an enemy ship in the midst of the ocean was the whole of life and a select body of them, the 'forlorn hope', stood poised in the bows of *San Felipe* as the vast galleon came up on the windward side of the *Revenge*. High up on the poop deck of *San Felipe* stood her captain, Don Claudio de Beamonte, a fine sight in his magnificent armour. At his command, trumpeters sounded the challenge and then, drawing his sword, he formally opened proceedings by calling on Sir Richard Grenville to surrender. 'Amaine for the King of Spain.' Sir Richard drew his sword in turn and saluted his enemy, but the challenge was answered only by the guns of the *Revenge*.

So big was *San Felipe* that, as she approached, her huge spread of canvas completely blanketed the *Revenge* and took all the wind out of the smaller galleon's sails, 'as the shippe could neither make way nor feel the helm, so huge and high carged [built] was the Spanish ship, being of a thousand and five hundreth tuns'. The Englishmen took one appalled look at their flapping sails and at the colossus hanging over them and then rushed for their arms as the beakhead of *San Felipe* crashed into the English galleon's side. As she struck, a Spanish sailor flung a rope round a convenient hitching post and ten bold men jumped down on to the deck of the *Revenge*.

At point-blank range, the starboard broadside of the *Revenge* opened fire. Her mighty lower-deck guns — culverins, demi-cannon and cannon-perrier — were horribly destructive at such a range and did serious damage to *San Felipe* above and below the waterline. Simultaneously, her upper battery was raking the decks of the Spanish galleon and attempting to destroy her masts and rigging, while musketeers directed their fire at the officers on the poop and through the open ports at the Spanish gunners. *San Felipe* reeled back at this bombardment, 'utterly misliking her first entertainment'. It was indeed, as the poet wrote, '*un cruel canonazo*', a savage demonstration of the might of English naval gunnery. Among those killed in this first salvo was one of the gentlemen adventurers from Lisbon, the noble Captain Don Jorge Troyano, 'who died well for his King', the first gentleman and possibly the first man to die in the battle of Flores.[10]

So sudden and so shattering was this first broadside from the *Revenge* that the sailors on *San Felipe* had no time to fix grappling irons on the English ship and the single rope holding the two galleons together parted under the strain as the ships recoiled from the gunfire. The two galleons 'fell asunder' and the soldiers and sailors of *San Felipe* watched in horror as clear water opened up between them and the ten men of the boarding party, now marooned on the decks of the *Revenge*, but prepared to sell their lives as dearly as possible.

At the moment of impact, those men on the *Revenge* not needed to work the guns or steer the ship had taken refuge in the strong-points in the half-deck and forecastle, the best places from which to clear the decks of boarders. But, now that the danger of wholesale invasion by the massed soldiers of *San Felipe* had passed, they abandoned cover and rushed towards the Spaniards who had dared to board a galleon of the Queen.

Ten men against a whole ship's company — an incident in the battle not even mentioned by English writers who were very reluctant to honour their enemies. These ten men fought bravely and well, but cut and thrust as they might their numbers were slowly reduced until there were only eight, then five and then just three men left, still fighting, still hoping for some miracle to save them.

That miracle now came up on the port side of the *Revenge* in the shape of Bertendona's *San Bernabe*. The three surviving soldiers fought their way towards her and, as *San Bernabe* struck, leaped upwards into the arms of their friends. These three brave men survived the battle and were suitably rewarded, 'since they have fought so valiantly and in order to give spirit to others who might follow their example on similar occasions'. The price of valour was '*seis scudos de ventaja*', six gold coins, the equivalent of about two months' pay for a Spanish sailor.[11]

Don Martín de Bertendona, old warrior that he was with his forty-five years' service on the sea, made sure that his ship would not fall asunder from the *Revenge*: 'I threw the grappling irons and ordered my galleon to be lashed to his.' Bertendona makes this manoeuvre sound simple in his letter to the King. He sailed alongside the *Revenge*, flung his grappling irons which immediately took a firm grip on the English galleon, and then ordered his sailors to lash the two ships together from stem to stern. But, of course, it can hardly have been as easy as this. At every stage of the proceedings, Englishmen were desperately trying to prevent Bertendona's orders from being carried out. A galleon like the *Revenge* relied in battle on the power of her guns, the strength of her construction, the skills and heart of her men and on her agility in evading close contact with the more heavily manned Spanish galleons. If Bertendona succeeded in lashing his ship to the *Revenge*, this last and most important English advantage would be lost.

One can imagine then that the sailors of *San Bernabe* had some difficulty in carrying out the orders of their commander. Like the men of *San Felipe* before them, they would have been on the receiving end of a broadside, or several broadsides, from the *Revenge*'s upper- and lower-deck batteries. And, as they worked totally exposed on the side of their ship, they were easy targets for the English soldiers and sailors in the fighting tops of the *Revenge* who rained down stones, arrows, musket shot and balls of fire, while their shipmates on deck fired hand-guns into the mass of Spaniards a few yards from them and hacked with swords at the hands of those trying to make the two galleons fast. Despite all this, the Spanish and Basque sailors on *San Bernabe* stuck to their task until it was completed. The *Revenge* and *San Bernabe* lay immobilized in the ocean, like two logs lashed together in a mastpond. And so they were to remain, hour after hour, '*costado con costado*', side by side, 'both of us fighting hard with cannon and arquebuses'.[12]

An older generation of naval historians tended to describe the *Revenge* hammering away at the Spaniards hour after hour with her big guns, a contest in which the Spaniards were at a pitiful disadvantage. 'The affair was miserably one-sided,' wrote Sir Geoffrey Callender, for instance. 'The heavy guns of the *Revenge*, magnificently handled, played havoc with the inferior craft that thus hardily stood up to her.'[13] This had happened in the great gun fight off the banks of Flanders in 1588 and it was for such a battle that the English galleon was designed, with guns strong enough to batter her opponents into submission and a ship handy and nimble enough to be able to stand back out of danger from Spanish attempts to close and board. But Sir Geoffrey had not read Bertendona's letter and so of course did not realize that the *Revenge* was actually lashed to a Spanish ship for all but the opening half-hour or so of the battle.

In such circumstances, would the English have been keen on using their heavy lower-deck broadside? This was designed ultimately to sink an enemy, but who would want to sink an enemy to whom one was so firmly manacled? In any case, how easy would it have been to fire the guns? Consider the manoeuvres necessary. Both ships had muzzle-loading guns in their lower-deck broadsides. For the Spaniards, reloading would have been virtually impossible for this was done outboard, the loader a few inches from the English ship. His task was to straddle the gun and, in this incredibly exposed position, sponge the barrel and replace the powder, wadding and shot. The English, with their more mobile gun-carriages, would have been in a better position since they could haul their guns back, slam their gunports shut and reload under cover. However, even this would have been difficult and very dangerous if one's ship was lashed to the enemy.[14]

Such considerations suggest that the English did not use their heavy guns to any great extent against *San Bernabe*, once she had succeeded in lashing herself to the *Revenge*. If they had, it seems impossible that the Apostle could have stayed afloat after hours and hours of battering at point-blank range by culverins and demi-cannon firing shot of between seventeen and thirty pounds' weight. As it was, the upper-works and decks of *San Bernabe* were badly damaged, but her hull does not seem to have been seriously holed by gunfire.

Corroboration that the *Revenge* did not fire her heavy guns very much in her last fight comes from the unusual circumstance that her gunpowder was recorded both before and after the battle. Readers of Raleigh and Tennyson will be surprised to hear that the *Revenge* had any gunpowder left at all. As every schoolboy of an earlier generation would have known, 'the powder was all of it spent'. But this is simply dramatic nonsense.[15] A Spanish inventory found seventy barrels of gunpowder left in the *Revenge* after the fight and, since she loaded ninety barrels in London, this means that just twenty barrels were expended in one of the fiercest and longest sea fights in naval history. If all this had been used by the twenty lower-deck guns, it would have been sufficient to fire them about seven or eight times each.[16] But, of course, powder was also consumed by the upper-deck battery, by muskets and by calivers, leaving even less for the great guns on the lower deck and so making it clear that the long fight between the *Revenge* and *San Bernabe* was not principally an artillery duel.

It was instead what contemporaries called a close fight, in this case a very close fight since the two ships were in contact with each other throughout the action. At this stage, it was a fairly even fight. *San Bernabe* was a rather bigger ship and had far more men, but the defender had all the advantages in a close fight. The *Revenge* no longer needed men to trim the sails or man the helm, for she was unable to move. Every fit man was thus available to defend the ship against boarders, though in fact Bertendona never attempted to board, no doubt thinking that attrition would do the job sooner or later. Boarding was by far the most dangerous and terrifying action in naval warfare, as Captain John Smith graphically informed his readers:

I confesse, the charging upon trenches, and the entrances of a breach in a
rampart are attempts as desperate as a man would thinke could be performed;
but he that hath tried himselfe as oft in the entring a resisting ship as I have
done . . . he would surely confesse there is no such dangerous service ashore
as a resolved, resolute fight at sea.[17]

Few men on the *Revenge* would have been visible to their enemies in
San Bernabe. Some were stationed in the forecastle, probably under the
command of Captain Langhorn. Others were in the half-deck below the
poop from where Sir Richard Grenville himself directed operations. Both
these strongholds were protected by very powerful bulwarks, the cubbridge-
heads as they were called. These had loopholes through which fire could be
directed on to the decks and sides of the ship from swivel-guns and hailshot
pieces, breech-loaders which could be rapidly reloaded by fitting a spare
chamber. These guns were supplemented by musketeers, so that one has
no trouble in believing Sir Richard Hawkins's description of another action:

What with our cubbridge heads, one answering the other . . . it was impossible to take us as long as any competent number of men had remained . . .
and for this, such shippes are called Impregnable, and are not to be taken,
but by surrender.[18]

More men were stationed amidships under the quarter-master, ready to
reinforce the forecastle or half-deck as necessary, and able to direct further
fire on the enemy from the loopholes in the hatch-coamings. Finally, high
up in the tops with a good store of missiles was a fourth body of fighting
sailors. These men were very vulnerable in such a close fight, though
they were protected to a certain extent by the wooden structure of the
tops themselves and by 'top armings'. These were awnings of red cloth
three-quarters of a yard high, which encircled the tops and were as much
for 'the countenance and grace of the ship as to cover the men from being
seen'. Cloth was small protection against musket fire, but it was better than
nothing and in any case the topmen had no choice but to stay where they
were, for descent was tantamount to suicide.

The day was drawing to a close as the two galleons lay locked in each other's murderous embrace. The sun was far down in the west and to the south the cliffs of Flores were barely to be seen. But it was to the north that the eyes of the men of the *Revenge* were turned in those moments when they were not watching *San Bernabe*. There, they could see more Spanish ships approaching, but beyond them nothing. Where was Lord Thomas Howard; where were the *Defiance* and the *Golden Lion* and the other galleons of the Queen? Surely they were not going to leave the *Revenge* to fight the whole Spanish armada alone?

When Lord Thomas saw the *Revenge* was trapped, according to Sir Walter Raleigh, he 'would have entered between the squadrons, but the rest would not condescend; and the master of his own ship offerred to leap into the sea rather than to conduct that Her Majesty's ship and the rest be a prey to the enemy.' Lord Thomas, in contrast to Grenville, bowed to his master's discretion and *Defiance* and most of the other ships of the English fleet kept well to windward of the Spaniards and 'gave divers volleys of shot and entered as far as the place permitted'.

Some individual ships were bolder. The *George Noble* of London was right alongside the *Revenge* when she was first attacked. Her captain asked Grenville 'what he would command him, being but one of the victuallers and of small force'. Sir Richard sensibly 'bid him save himself and leave him to his fortune'. More valuable assistance was provided by the *Foresight*, the smallest of the Queen's galleons in Lord Thomas's fleet. Her brave captain, Thomas Vavasour, 'performed a very great fight and stayed two hours near the *Revenge* as the weather would permit him, not forsaking the fight till he was like to be encompassed by the squadrons'. Now, threatened with the same fate as the *Revenge*, he twisted and turned 'and with very great difficulty cleared himself'.

Spanish evidence does not support Raleigh's description of this limited assistance to the *Revenge*. Don Alonso de Bazán, in his official *relación*, reported no offensive action from Howard and the other English ships after the initial exchange of gunfire as the English broke through between the squadrons and took the windward station. The Spanish Captain-General claimed that he chased the English fleet until they were obscured by the night, 'spattering them with gunfire and doing great damage'. The last that was seen of them, they were fleeing in disorder, 'some making off to the westward, some towards the islands under cover of darkness, others by various routes, whereof we have so far no news'.

As usual, the truth no doubt lies somewhere between these two accounts. The English fleet certainly did escape into the obscurity and safety of the night, leaving the *Revenge* to her plight. However, it seems unlikely that Lord Thomas's ships, safe on the windward station, did nothing at all to assist Sir Richard's galleon. As for the damage done to the English by Bazán's ships, this needs to be taken with a pinch of salt since there is no English evidence to support it. Don Alonso, like Lord Thomas Howard, was in trouble after the battle for not having achieved more; in his case, for not having captured the whole English fleet at anchor. It is therefore not surprising to find him claiming considerable damage to the fleeing ships and even suggesting, with no evidence whatsoever, that the *Defiance*, 'the worst sailer amongst them', was so badly holed that she wrecked the next day on the coast of the island of São Jorge.

And so there was to be no help for the *Revenge*. As night fell, Sir Richard and his men were left to fight alone. The wind was still from the east and the open sea between Flores and Corvo was probably quite choppy as Don Alonso de Bazán returned from his pursuit of Howard to 'give heart' to Bertendona. The soldiers and sailors in the galleons of Spain eagerly awaited the moment of truth as they closed in on Sir Richard Grenville, 'the bellowing, fierce bull . . . the brave bull that was so full of blood and courage'.[19]

CHAPTER TWELVE

AND THE WHOLE
OF THE NIGHT

'And the sun went down, and the stars
came out far over the summer sea,
But never a moment ceased the fight
of the one and the fifty-three.

T ENNYSON'S 'STARS' may well be poetic licence for, according to the
Spanish evidence, it was a very dark night. There was no moon and
the only illumination came from balls of fire and from the flashes of guns
and muskets on board *San Bernabe* and the *Revenge*. This deadly firework
display must have had a strange beauty for those thousands of Spanish
soldiers and sailors who viewed it through the eleven hours of darkness
and death which elapsed before sunrise on the last day of August 1591.[1]
The men of the *Revenge* were to have little time for beauty, but they all
knew it was going to be a very long night, a night without sleep unless it
was for ever.

So far the battle had not gone too badly for the *Revenge*. Her guns had
hit the great *San Felipe* so hard that the Spanish galleon had withdrawn
from the fray and was to play no further part in the battle. She had not
foundered, as Raleigh suggested, but she was badly damaged. The English
ship had also held its own in the slugging match with *San Bernabe*. The
upper-works of both galleons were scarred and splintered and the *Revenge*
may already have lost some spars, perhaps even a mast. But the defensive
positions in the half-deck and forecastle were still sound and few men had
yet been killed or wounded.

It was then with profound thanks for small mercies that the English
sang their evening psalm. It seemed unlikely that many would see the
dawn. Fighting in daylight was exhausting and dangerous, but at least

Within the image: George Clifford Earle of Cumberland . 1588

PLATE 12 *George Clifford, 3rd Earl of Cumberland,*
after Nicholas Hilliard, c.1590.

PLATE 13 *Frontispiece of* The Mariners Mirrour
(1588) engraved by Theodor de Bry.

one could see the enemy if he tried to board one's ship. To fight at night was quite another matter, an eerie and very frightening experience. Tired eyes struggled to keep alert for the approach of boarders through the gloom. Ears were pricked to distinguish the noise of muffled oars or an approaching galleon from the cacophony of gunfire, screams and the never-ending symphony of drums and trumpets on the afterdeck of *San Bernabe*. Here, near the poop lantern, the galleon's six trumpeters played 'loudly and continuously to animate their shipmates and strike terror into the enemy'.[2]

Darkness made it safer to move about the ship. Sir Richard Grenville could make the rounds to hearten his men and urge them to fight on. Time might now be found to prepare a meal to help the weary soldiers and sailors to get through the night. And perhaps, after having been so recently ashore, the cook could serve something fresh. The rabbits, chicken and lamb for which Flores was famous would have made a pleasant change from the remaining foul victuals sent out from London. And maybe the men could fight rather better on the local wine than on stale beer. 'A health to you all, fore and aft. Courage, my hearts, for a fresh charge.'[3]

The Spanish were avid to seize the galleon in their grasp and a fresh charge soon came. This seems to have taken the men of the *Revenge* by surprise. Perhaps they were so busy peering at *San Bernabe* through the murk that they were slow to notice danger coming from a different direction. But Bertendona in *San Bernabe* made no attempt to board, fearing the confusion likely to arise from 'the darkness of the night'. Such fears were not shared by Marcos de Aramburu who now came up to join the fray in *San Cristóbal*. His approach was so stealthy that the first the English knew of it was when he rammed the *Revenge* in the stern with his beakhead, from which a picked party of soldiers climbed on to the English galleon's poop.

A desperate hand-to-hand fight ensued, with Sir Richard himself in the thick of it. Steel clashed with steel under the light of the poop lantern, as Grenville's men fought savagely to clear the ship of boarders. But this fight favoured the Spanish who gradually drove the English back with weight of numbers and the impetus of their attack. More and more soldiers poured on to the stern of the *Revenge*. With musket fire and push of pike they killed several of the English defenders and wounded many more, including Sir Richard Grenville himself who received a musket ball in his body. '*Victoria, victoria*' screamed the Spaniards as they seized the ensign from the poop and brandished it aloft in triumph. Step by step, the Englishmen were forced back, down off the poop and then right back to the mainmast.

But now the tide turned. Sir Richard ordered his men to take cover below, a move which left the Spaniards open to the massed fire of the Englishmen in the forecastle whose view had previously been obstructed by the retreating backs of their mates. This volley proved decisive. The Spanish were rolled back, their retreat hastened as Grenville's men rose again from cover and slaughtered many of their enemies as the Spaniards raced to leap back on to *San Cristóbal*. She was not quite the same ship that they had left only a few minutes before. While the men on the poop were fighting with the Spanish soldiers, below them in the gun-room the two big culverins of the stern chase had been smashing into the bows of *San Cristóbal*. These guns were very nearly touching the Spanish ship and the damage they did was terrible to see. The whole of her bows right down to the waterline were smashed to pieces and Aramburu had no choice but to disengage before his galleon sank. As he sheered off, lanterns were lit and grouped together as a signal for other ships to come to his assistance.

For Grenville and the *Revenge* this assault by the soldiers of *San Cristóbal* had been a very close thing. They had lost control of the poop and quarter-deck and had their ensign captured, but Grenville's men, that 'tag and rag' of pressed men, had stood firm and fought bravely to free the *Revenge* of boarders. However, there were now fewer men to defend her as the toll of dead and wounded rose. The wounds received in a close fight were horrible: gunshot wounds, burns, splinters and the gashes of cold steel. 'I was so hurt and bruised,' exclaimed a deponent in another fight. 'I was shot into the mouth, thrust into the leg with a pike, hurt with a splinter in my left hand and so bruised with a great stone on my right thigh.'[4] Many men in the *Revenge* were wounded as many times as this deponent; some even more. The master, for instance, that man who had wanted to run before the fight, 'had at the least ten or twelve wounds, as well in his head as in his body'. Nor were matters any better in *San Bernabe* as Bertendona reported later to the King: 'There are few who were not burned by fire or wounded, either a little or a lot, and others dead.'[5]

These Spanish wounded could benefit from spiritual succour not available on the *Revenge*. Those chaplains, for whom King Philip had scoured Spain, stood at the opening of the hatchway below decks with the surgeon. Here they received and comforted the wounded, took their confessions and gave the last rites to those whom the surgeons could not save. The *Revenge* had no chaplain and her crew had to look to each other for such services: 'Then we (one and all) prayed unto the Lord to blesse us . . . and so we forgave one another and went to the battle.'[6]

Comfort and prayer might well do more good to the wounded than could the surgeons who, however willing, were severely restricted by the contemporary state of their art. The status of surgeons was low and that of sea surgeons lowest of all, but even the most able could not hope for much success in a world in which it was hoped that the pain of a very tight tourniquet would 'greatly obscure the sense and feeling' of an amputation. But sailormen were hardy folk and many were cured.

Successful amputations were carried out by candlelight in the heaving holds of ships, bones were set, wounds probed and cleaned and bullets and arrow-heads successfully extracted. Revolting ointments and poultices were applied to burns and they still healed up. The contents of the contemporary surgeon's chest might seem to belong to a museum of horrors, but those saws and crane's-bill pincers, probes and knives and cauterizing irons, those unguents, syrups, pills and plasters quite often cured the wounded men brought down below for the attention of the surgeon and his mates.[7]

Such relief for the wounded of the *Revenge* was not to last much longer. Common sense determined that the surgeon's station was in the hold, 'where he should be in no danger of shot; for there cannot be a greater disheartening of the company than in his miscarrying, whereby they will be deprived of all help for hurt and wounded men.'[8] But, when Sir Richard Grenville was wounded in the fight on the poop, he refused to go below and the surgeon had to come on deck to attend to him. While dressing Sir Richard's wound in this exposed position, he was shot and shortly afterwards died of his wounds. Sir Richard, too, was hit again by the same volley, suffering this time a very nasty head wound which bled profusely but did not reduce either his pride or his determination never to surrender.

The wounded commander continued to urge his men to fight on. And fight on they did, as did the men of *San Bernabe*. They still made no attempt to board the *Revenge*, but their firepower was beginning to have a serious effect. More Englishmen were killed, while the upper-works of the *Revenge* were gradually being reduced to a shambles. Bertendona was to honour his brave men in letters to the King, praising their valiant and long-drawn-out fight. A few were singled out for particular praise, such as his gallant son Juan who was twenty-four years old and 'fought very well' and two fighting Irishmen — Sir Charles O'Connor and Sir Robert Laso, who 'showed great valour in this *jornada*' — two among many of their countrymen in the Spanish fleet who were just as happy to fight the English in the waters of the Azores as in the bogs of Munster.[9]

These valiant men did not have to fight the *Revenge* single-handed for very much longer. *San Cristóbal*'s signal for assistance was seen and another galleon from the squadron of Castile came up to join the fight. This was the 530-ton *Asunción*, 'one of the King's old galleons'. She was commanded by Don Antonio Manrique and her soldiers led by Pedro de Pliego.[10] Manrique steered his ship into the gap between the bows of the *Revenge* and those of *San Bernabe* and so opened up a new point of attack on the English galleon. The place of his assault must have seemed well chosen since the bows were singled out by a contemporary expert as 'the best and safest boarding for entering [an enemy ship]'. Once the grapples had been flung and fastened, this is just what Pedro de Pliego and his soldiers did.

The Spanish were however in a very exposed position on the beakhead and the bows of the *Revenge*, only a few feet from the forecastle, the most strongly defended position in the ship. The Englishmen greeted these new arrivals with a hail of musket bullets and case-shot. Try as they might, the Spaniards could make no further progress into the ship. Those not shot were routed by push of pike and the sword and driven back into their own ship or into the sea. The defenders of the forecastle breathed again, but knew that this assault would be but the first of many, since *Asunción* could easily be reinforced from *San Bernabe* and from other ships coming up in the lee of Bertendona's galleon. Failure to take the *Revenge* would not come from dearth of men, since Don Alonso had 4,000 soldiers in his fleet, not to mention the sailors, surely enough to defeat the 200 or so men still left defending the *Revenge*.

And now came yet another assailant, the fifth ship from the Spanish fleet to run alongside the *Revenge*. Dom Luis de Coutinho, commander of the flyboats, had watched the battle from afar and could no longer bear to be out of the action. His zeal was greater than his seamanship. He came through the dark 'in a great hurry' in *La Serena*, flagship of his squadron, and rammed and holed the *Asunción* as he ran alongside her. This accident did nothing to dampen his ardour. He grappled the bows of the *Revenge* and he too flung men on to the English galleon, but once again the defence from the forecastle was too strong and they were driven back.

Three enemy ships were now fastened securely to the *Revenge*, two on her bows and one fixed stem to stern on her port side — a floating battlefield 'not able to move one way or other, but . . . with the waves and billows of the sea'. The time was now about midnight and the darkness remained impenetrable save for the fires on the four fighting ships. In these black graveyard hours, the fight went on and on. Time and time again, men from *Asunción* or *La Serena* managed to set foot on the bows of the *Revenge*, only to be repulsed once more by the defenders in the forecastle who were well supplied with ammunition from the powder magazine just below them. And so the rhythm of the fight went on through the early hours of the morning — attack, repulse and then a lull, sometimes short, sometimes longer, providing time for a drink and perhaps a psalm or two before the next attack. There was no denying the courage of these Spaniards and Portuguese as they tried 'to force her by the multitudes of their armed soldiers and musketeers, but were still repulsed again and again, and at all times beaten back into their own ships, or into the sea'.

How many times the men from *Asunción* and *La Serena* tried to board is not recorded. Once they nearly covered the short distance to the forecastle before being cut down, but usually they did not get so far before being forced to give up each fresh attempt. There was no way into the *Revenge* through her bows as the English fought on, hour after hour, with no chance to succour their wounded or to 'winde up the slaine, with each a weight or bullet at their heads and feet to make them sinke, and give them three guns for their funerals'.[11] The English dead lay where they fell and their guns were put to better use.

While the forecastle of the *Revenge* stood against each successive assault, the gunners on the three Spanish ships were hitting the English galleon with telling effect. One after another, the three masts of the *Revenge* came tumbling down and with them the flags and banners and the battered red cross of Saint George and England. No longer were there any fighting tops from which defenders could hurl down stones and balls of fire on their assailants. The decks were littered with broken yards and cables and sails, a terrible clutter increasing the confusion ever present in the dark night. Worse still, the pounding was removing the superstructure. The poop and quarter-deck which had seen the great fight with the men from *San Cristóbal* were no more, smashed to pieces by the Spanish guns. Soon, there were great rents in the cubbridge-heads of the half-deck and forecastle where the dwindling numbers of defenders were concentrated. There was much damage too below the waterline and the carpenter and his mates strove manfully to patch up each new hole as it appeared, while the sick men on the ballast must have wondered if this really was the safest place in the ship as the water rose towards them. As his ship crumbled about him and his men died, Sir Richard Grenville stood proud, sword in hand and his face a bloody mask from the wound in his head. 'Fight on! Fight on!' he cried. 'No surrender!'

With three Spanish ships all firing at such close quarters, they risked damaging each other as well as the *Revenge*. Dom Luis Coutinho had already holed the *Asunción* with his impetuous arrival on the battle scene and these two ships were to do further damage to each other. But the greatest danger was to Bertendona's men in *San Bernabe* whose midships and stern were in the direct line of fire and likely to be hit if the guns were elevated too much. This happened several times and added to the damage done by the *Revenge*, one 'friendly' shot killing Luis de San Juan, the captain of the soldiers and the noblest Spanish victim of the battle.

He was a particular friend of Bertendona, who recorded his death with great emotion in a letter to the King whom he begged to look after San Juan's mother and his two daughters:

> for whom there is no help apart from the Almighty and Your Majesty . . . He when dying, charged me to report this . . . and I beg you to believe that, with his stomach laid open and his breast bare, with the greatest courage he asked me to tell Your Majesty with what contentment he died on such an occasion serving Your Majesty.

Hundreds of men died in this battle, but only this one death was recorded in such detail.

The big guns of the *Revenge* were not completely quiet during this stage of the battle, for the two great cannon in her bows could be brought to bear on her most recent assailants. These did great damage, so much so that in the early hours of the morning the *Asunción*, already holed by Dom Luis, began to settle deeper into the water and then quite suddenly sank at the side of the *Revenge*. Her captain, Don Antonio Manrique, managed to escape on to Bertendona's galleon with many of his men, but at least a hundred of her crew were lost, either already dead from the battle or drowned as she went to the bottom. *La Serena* was in nearly as bad a condition. Holed several times by the guns of the *Revenge*, she was to sink the next day, her men safely evacuated before she went down to join *Asunción* on the sea bed.

Spanish accounts of the battle make it clear that only five ships actually ran alongside the *Revenge* to fight the close fight. Linschoten, however, who talked to English survivors after the battle, said that 'with seven or eight ships they boarded her, but she withstood them all.' Sir Walter Raleigh doubled this figure in his account: 'So that ere the morning . . . there had fifteen several armadas assailed her . . . besides those which beat her at large', that is fired at the *Revenge* from a distance. Both writers may have exaggerated — in Raleigh's case, this seems certainly so. But the differing reports may reflect a change of tactics by the Spaniards, now seriously alarmed by the damage done to all five ships which had closed with the *Revenge*.

Don Alonso de Bazán described himself as sailing in *San Pablo* from one side to the other of the battle, marshalling his ships around the four grappled together in their deadly fight. The Spanish fleet thus formed a ring around the *Revenge* at a safe distance from her guns, a difficult manoeuvre on a dark night. According to Bazán, soldiers were poured into the *Revenge* 'without cessation' throughout the night 'amid all the risks of confusion due to the darkness'. Whence came all these soldiers? Did they all board from *Asunción* and *La Serena*? This seems a little unlikely, since this approach had proved to be so well defended. As long as there was powder and ball in the forecastle, the English could check any number of assaults from this direction. But English numbers were very limited and falling by the hour, so that it would have severely stretched them to defend against attacks from more than one direction.

Maybe Don Alonso did attack the *Revenge* from directions other than her bows, perhaps sending men in boats from the encircling galleons to try to board her in the stern or on her starboard quarter, as one historian has suggested.[12] This would explain why Linschoten and Raleigh reported that the *Revenge* was assaulted by men from more than five Spanish ships. But if Don Alonso did change his tactics in this way, these boatloads of soldiers were no more successful than those who had boarded her on to the poop and in the bows. Many Spaniards set their feet on the *Revenge* during those long hours of darkness, but none stayed there very long, unless they were dead or so badly wounded that they could no longer scramble back to safety. No wonder Spaniards later said that Sir Richard Grenville and all his company were 'the most valiantest people that was possible to meet withal in combat'.[13]

Although exhausted after some fourteen hours of continuous close-range combat, eleven of them through the obscurity of the night, the defenders stood firm. All attempts to board the galleon were defeated by the stubborn resistance of her dwindling band of men and by Sir Richard Grenville who 'immortalized himself by a defence such as has never, either before or since, been witnessed upon the sea'.[14] Few would doubt that. Sir Richard's leadership, determination and example were an inspiration to those he commanded. But it would be unjust to forget these mainly anonymous men, 'a small troop to man such a ship and a weak garrison to resist so mighty an army'.[15]

Sailors were often derided for their mercenary attitude to their service, for being interested in nothing beyond their pay and especially the prize money they could gain. But such criticism was unfair to the mariners of England. They had a code of conduct in action which was far from mercenary in its determination to fight on against all odds. Cowardice was despised, as a later captain discovered when accused by his crew of not giving his all. How dare a captain hold back, his men exclaimed, when they were prepared 'to spend their lives and limbs in this service for the good of our native country of England'. Such were the men of the *Revenge*.[16]

The emotions and thoughts of these men of the *Revenge* during her last terrible battle are unknown, for no documents written by anyone on board have survived, though some were written. William Langhorn, for instance, the unsung captain of the forecastle who survived the battle unscathed, 'wrote a letter wherein he declared all the manner of the fight', but that letter is sadly lost. And Philip Gawdy, whose letters to his brother so vividly record the voyage out to the Azores, 'kept a note of every day's action which by God's grace you shall be acquainted with'. Philip also survived, but his notes did not, and so we do not know how he described this day and night of action, nor what he thought as the darkness diminished in the east and he could just make out the piled corpses of his shipmates. He had been proud of his good armour and his shield, as good 'as any man that goeth in our voyage'. He had hoped 'to winne much honour' in the *Revenge*, but he can hardly have imagined that he would have had to win it in such a desperate fight as this. 'God of battles, was ever a battle like this in the world before?'[17]

CHAPTER THIRTEEN

AT BREAK OF DAY

Bendita sea la luz
y la Santa Veracruz . . .
Bendito sea el dia
y el señor que nos le envia.

Blessed be the light,
and the Holy True Cross . . .
Blessed be the day,
and the Lord who sends it to us.[1]

THE STRAINS OF the morning prayer rising from the decks of the Spanish fleet brought mixed feelings to the remaining men of the *Revenge*. They had survived the night, a blessing for which they could thank God in their turn. But how could they possibly survive the day? No longer did any Spaniard dare to stand and fight on the decks of the *Revenge*, but there were thousands near to hand, ready to close in for the kill. *San Bernabe* and *La Serena* still remained firmly shackled to the English ship, while all around lay galleon after galleon as far as the eye could see.

And the Spanish fleet with broken sides
lay round us all in a ring;
But they dared not touch us again, for they
fear'd that we still could sting,
So they watch'd what the end would be.[2]

Among these Spanish galleons was one small English ship, the faithful *Pilgrim* which 'had hovered all night to see the success'. Now plainly visible to her enemies, she 'was hunted like a hare amongst many ravenous houndes . . . but escaped'.

What hope of escape was there for the *Revenge*? She now lay very low in the water 'like a logge on the seas'. The once beautiful galleon had been reduced to a complete shambles, 'the mastes all beaten over board, all her tackle cut asunder, her upper worke altogether rased, and in effect evened she was with the water, but the very foundation or bottom of a ship, nothing being left over head either for flight or defence.' She was a shambles too in the literal sense, 'the hatches begored with blood, and strowed with slain carcases and men half dead . . . a sad and doleful spectacle to them that were left alive.'[3] What devil dwelt in the hearts of Englishmen that so battered a ship could so long resist an armada and still show no sign of surrender?

'As the day encreased, so our men decreased,' wrote Sir Walter Raleigh. 'And, as the light grew more and more, by so much more grew our discomforts.' The Englishmen had fought bravely through the night, but dawn removed their most effective defence. As the sun rose, they became easy prey with only the shell of the forecastle and half-deck to protect them. Now surely was the time for surrender with honour, with further resistance virtually impossible. Surrender might well mean loss of liberty, perhaps a long time on the benches of a Spanish galley, but did not even that seem preferable to almost certain death?

How many men were left alive to think such thoughts? Raleigh, rather surprisingly, puts the number of dead relatively low — 'fortie of her best men slaine and the most part of the rest hurt'. This was out of his total numbers of 190 of whom 90 had been too sick to fight, almost certainly too low a total as has been seen. Linschoten said that 'of the English were slaine about a hundred.' The Spanish authorities, however, give much higher numbers of dead and they were to be in a better position to count. Don Alonso de Bazán, in his official *relación*, said there were 250 men on the *Revenge* of whom 'were left one hundred', a number confirmed by Cabrera de Córdoba who wrote that the English lost 150 dead 'and most of those that remained were wounded'. Don Juan de Maldonado, Inspector-General of the Spanish fleet, a man whose job it was to count things accurately, put the loss even higher and said there were only 80 Englishmen left alive after the battle, though this figure may reflect men who died later from their wounds.[4]

The men of the *Revenge* had thus paid very dearly for their long, long fight against such overwhelming numbers. At least 150 men out of the crew of 250, or 60 per cent, had been killed. Most of the rest had been wounded, many several times and some so badly that they would later die. A 'butcher's bill' of this magnitude would have convinced the most implacable court-martial of Nelson's day that it was long past time for Sir Richard Grenville to have hauled down his flag, if he had still had a mast from which to fly one.

But Sir Richard was now as determined not to surrender as he had been not to run away the previous afternoon.[5] Though now very weak from his head wound and barely able to stand, he was still able to summon up fresh strength to make one last effort to deny his ship to Spain. There was one way left — a desperate, terrible and self-destructive way — to set a match to the gunpowder and blow up his ship. Such a threat was well known among beleaguered seamen, especially the Dutch, but in Grenville's case it was unlikely to be just a threat. Sir Richard was a man of his word and, with seventy barrels of powder left, he had the means to send to kingdom come not only his own ship but also those which grappled him.

He called the remaining men of his company together and praised them for their courage and heart during the great fight. He then persuaded them, 'or as many as he could induce, to yield themselves unto God, and to the mercy of none else; but as they had, like valiant resolute men, repulsed so many enemies, they should not now shorten the honour of their nation by prolonging their own lives for a few hours or a few days.' The Spaniards, he said, 'should never glory to have taken one ship of Her Majesty, seeing they had so long and so notably defended themselves'. Sir Richard then gave the order so stirringly interpreted by Tennyson:

Sink me the ship, Master Gunner —
sink her, split her in twain!
Fall into the hands of God,
not into the hands of Spain!

Grenville's eloquence was sufficient to persuade a substantial number of those who heard him that it was indeed their duty to commit suicide for the glory and honour of God, St George and the Queen. The master gunner himself 'readily condescended and divers others'.

But Captain Langhorn and the master, the two most senior men after Grenville, 'were of another opinion' and checked the gunner from carrying out his order. They put the case of survival. They had all fought long and well, they said, and might do so again, 'there being divers sufficient and valiant men yet living [who] might do their country and prince acceptable service hereafter.' The duty of such men was to 'live to fight again and to strike another blow'. The Spaniards, they assured their shipmates, would be 'ready to entertain a composition', to allow them to surrender with honour and with the promise of liberty. As for the *Revenge* herself, she would never fly the flag of Spain: 'With the first working of the sea, she must needs sink, and was besides so crushed and bruised as she could never be removed out of the place.'

The passionate argument continued on the stricken galleon. Sir Richard, furious in mind but steadily weakening in body, refused to countenance the reasoned arguments of Captain Langhorn and continued to insist that a match be set to the serried casks of powder in the magazine below. But the captain, with his promise of life and liberty, 'won unto him the greater party'. Meanwhile, the master had himself conveyed to the Spanish flagship to put his proposition to Don Alonso in person. He was a tragic sight with his 'ten or twelve wounds' and the case he made was utterly persuasive. Don Alonso could have no doubt what the master meant when he emphasized the 'dangerous disposition' of Sir Richard Grenville.

Don Alonso did not take long to make up his mind. He had already lost one fine galleon in this fight, was just about to lose the flyboat *La Serena* and had three other galleons very seriously damaged by the firepower of the *Revenge*, not to mention less serious damage to many other ships in his fleet. He had also lost several hundred men dead or drowned and many more wounded by the desperate resistance of the Englishmen.[6] He had no wish to lose any more ships or men. Now he could bring the affair to a satisfactory conclusion. He would have the honour of capturing the *Revenge* and of saving the lives, not only of his own men, but also of those brave enemies who had

141

so stoutly fought against him under their noble commander, Sir Richard Grenville, 'whom for his notable valour he seemed greatly to honour and admire'.

He therefore agreed with the master of the *Revenge* that the English ship should be surrendered 'by composition'. The lives of all on board would be spared, 'the company sent for England, and the better sort to pay such reasonable ransom as their estate would bear, and in the mean season to be free from galley or imprisonment'. These are Sir Walter Raleigh's words, but they can be confirmed from Spanish sources. Don Alonso did not mention the 'composition' in his official *relación*, nor did he and his squadron commanders mention it in their reports to the King. It was after all rather shameful to report that a whole armada had been able to capture just one English ship only on such advantageous conditions to the enemy. But they admitted it elsewhere. Bertendona, in his initial report on the campaign, said merely that he fought the *Revenge* 'for the rest of the day and the whole of the night until the morning, when I captured her'. But in a later letter, he confirmed the truth of Raleigh's melodramatic account of the end of the battle. He explained that, contrary to normal practice, the English prisoners were treated well because they had threatened 'to burn their ship and send it to the bottom together with themselves and with the ships of the King'.[7] Raleigh did not invent the story for dramatic effect. Sir Richard Grenville really had intended to send his ship and his men 'into the hands of God, not into the hands of Spain'.

Many of his men believed that he might still do this, even after the master returned with the news of the composition. This was greeted with profound relief, even by most of those who previously had cheered Sir Richard's audacious order to the master gunner. They now 'drew back from Sir Richard and the Master gunner, being no hard matter to dissuade men from death to life'. But Grenville still did not waver in his determination and 'divers of our men, fearing Sir Richard's disposition, stole away' on boats which took them to *San Pablo* and other ships in the Spanish fleet. Others still wanted to die rather than surrender. The master gunner himself, thwarted of his master stroke, drew his sword and would have slain himself, 'had he not been by force withheld and locked into his cabin'. And Sir Richard, now at the limits of pain and grief and no longer able to stand, looked on with dying disdain at those who preferred life and liberty to honour. His strength finally failed him and he had to be carried aboard *San Pablo*. As he left the *Revenge*, he fainted from the pain and then, in a brief moment of consciousness, 'desired the company to pray for him'.

As the English prisoners were scattered among the ships of the Spanish fleet, so the victors came to admire their prize. They had to pick their way carefully through the wreckage and the carnage, 'the ship being marvellous unsavoury, filled with blood and bodies of dead and wounded men like a slaughter house.' Almost at once, there was dispute as to whom should fall the honour of having captured the first ship of the Queen ever taken by Spain. Don Martín de Bertendona was in no doubt that the honour should be his. Was it not he who had grappled the English galleon at the beginning of the battle and had clung on hour after hour until the end? 'I captured her,' he wrote with pride in his letter to the King. But his claim was justly challenged by Dom Luis Coutinho in *La Serena* who, although not the first to close with the *Revenge*, had made more attempts to capture the stronghold of her forecastle than anyone else.[8]

The quarrel between Bertendona and Coutinho was taken up by their men, a heated dispute inflamed by the fact that the men of *San Bernabe* were Basques and those of *La Serena* mainly Portuguese. Hands were on swords and daggers and 'there had almost a new fight arisen betweene the Biscaines and the Portingales: while each of them would have the honour to have first boarded her.' This fresh fight was quelled in time and honour partially satisfied as the various flags and ensigns of the *Revenge* were grabbed by each party as trophies to prove that it was indeed they who had captured the famed English galleon.[9]

Don Alonso himself was tactful in his distribution of praise. In a letter to the King, he recommended that honour and thanks be given to Bertendona, Coutinho and Aramburu — in that order in the letter, if not in degree of valour. Aramburu, it will be remembered, had fought the fight on the poop and his men too had an ensign to remind them of that moment of glory. Don Alonso also asked the King to honour Don Claudio de Beamonte, captain of *San Felipe*, and Don Antonio Manrique, commander of the sunken *Asunción*, so all five of the commanders who brought their galleons alongside the *Revenge* received thanks for their courage and dedication to duty. What material rewards they received is not clear, though it seems that Bertendona got, among other things, 'a gold chain with a whistle worth 100 ducats'.[10]

But all this lay far in the future. For the moment, their quarrel settled, the victors could savour their triumph and admire the great galleon they had captured: It was a Spanish maxim that 'the greater the vanquished the more honour to the victor', so one can perhaps take their praise of the *Revenge* with a little pinch of salt.[11] Nevertheless, that praise seems genuine enough and their awesome appreciation of the might and grace of the English ship rings true after 400 years. Don Martín de Bertendona thought her 'one of the finest galleons in the world', even in the stricken state in which he viewed her, and reported that the ship with her guns, ammunition and stores was said to be worth over 80,000 ducats, or £27,500, a fine prize indeed. Falcão de Resende described in his poem how the victors admired 'the structure and the build' of the vanquished galleon with her cargo of corpses. He also noted some other cargo which might have surprised those investors in London who had received reports of the capture only of such mundane goods as sugar and hides: 'And there, amongst other booty, was fine silver and gold which our prudent Bazán took away into safe keeping.'[12]

However, it was the guns of the *Revenge* which most impressed her captors, 'the finest artillery which has ever been seen in a sailing ship', according to Bertendona. Don Juan de Maldonado confirmed the quality of the guns and noted that they were 'for the most part cast in England', suggesting that some of them had been acquired elsewhere by purchase or capture. Don Alonso was equally admiring:

> She carried forty-two pieces of bronze ordnance; or rather, all but three which she had transferred to another ship in the squadron a few days earlier. The twenty on the lower deck were of 40 to 60 quintals; the other twenty-two between 20 and 30 quintals, — all in good condition.[13]

If these figures were accurate, the *Revenge* was carrying a staggering amount of metal and it is not surprising that the Spaniards were impressed. There is no gun weighing over 50 quintals in a list of the artillery in the Spanish fleet drawn up while they were in Ferrol. A few demi-cannon, culverins and demi-culverins were over 40 quintals, but these were very much the exception, the typical weight of these guns being between 20 and 40 quintals. The weight given by Bazán for the upper-deck guns of the *Revenge* is equally surprising. Demi-culverins would normally fall into the range of 20 to 30 quintals, a few being heavier, but it was fairly unusual for the smaller type of demi-culverin known as a saker to be over 20 quintals and almost unheard of for a demi-saker or falconet to be of this weight. One's suspicions that Don Alonso was exaggerating in the flush of victory are confirmed by another document in the Spanish archives which records the weights of some of the upper-deck guns of the *Revenge* after they had been carried back to Lisbon. The weights in this list are a little ambiguous, but at face value they are recorded in quintals and they show that, of the eleven guns whose weights were listed, only three were over 20 quintals.[14]

The Spaniards may have exaggerated the merits of their prize a little, but it was still a wonderful trophy and they were desperately keen to get it back to Spain so that the whole world could appreciate their triumph. When Captain Langhorn persuaded the men to surrender, he had said that the *Revenge* would sink in the first heavy seas. After a survey of the damage, the Spanish thought otherwise. Two days after the battle, a working party was sent aboard under the command of Don Antonio de Urquiola to lighten the ship by taking out her ammunition, powder and guns and to repair her sufficiently to get to Spain. The weather prevented him from taking off the heavy lower-deck guns, but seventeen of those on the upper deck and the seventy remaining casks of gunpowder were transferred to *San Pablo* while his working party set to their task. Spanish fleets were well equipped for such work. They all carried divers for repairs under water and these, working in conjunction with carpenters inside, were able to plug the holes made during the battle. Meanwhile, spare masts were transferred to the *Revenge* and men set about the long task of rerigging her. The *Revenge* began to look like a galleon again.[15]

The men of the *Revenge* were also patched up as far as possible by their Spanish captors, who seem to have honoured the spirit of the composition and treated them with kindness. Don Juan de Maldonado described the prisoners as 'people of little account, although in general good sailors and gunners', certainly good enough for the service of Spain. Raleigh reported an attempt by an Irish exile to recruit some of these Englishmen for the Spanish navy. He promised that their pay would be trebled and there would be the chance of 'advancement to the better sort'. Raleigh, in a long diatribe, threw scorn on such promises by 'a notable traitor', but it is clear that at least some of the men from the *Revenge* paid heed to them. Thomas Meade of Devon, a former seaman on the *Revenge* who reached Dartmouth on 13 November, reported the defection of 'divers English gunners who serve the King'. In the short list of names are such turncoats as William Bussell of Newcastle and the Welshman William Jones, both of whom had transferred their skills to *San Felipe*, that great Apostle which they had so severely battered only a few months earlier.[16]

Service in the Spanish navy did not however attract many of the men of the *Revenge* and those who survived their wounds were returned home as promised. When Don Alonso reached Lisbon, he begged the King to make arrangements for the English prisoners to be granted their liberty, a plea which received the royal assent. In November, Bertendona reported that Don Alonso had determined, in agreement with his council, to treat the prisoners well and send them back to their homeland. In the same month, Bazán was arranging for them to be put on ships sailing to England. And so they trickled back home, these anonymous heroes. None have left any account of their adventures although, for the rest of their lives, they no doubt regaled their families and friends with stories of the fight. These survivors of the *Revenge* were not entirely forgotten by the Queen who, 'of her free grace', ordered that they should receive as reward for their good service 'every one his six months' wages'.[17]

The terms of surrender had provided for 'the better sort to pay such reasonable ransom as their estate would bear', a fruit of battle often very profitable to the victor. In the case of the *Revenge*, however, the haul was to prove disappointing for it was discovered on enquiry that the English galleon carried very few 'persons of consequence'. There was one who was 'bred to the sea who died of his wounds', a description which fits the much injured master who died on the way back to Spain. Three other possible objects of ransom were given by Don Alonso to Bertendona as some reward for his services, a gift which was accompanied by a request to treat the prisoners as well as they had been aboard his own flagship.[18]

These three men were Captain Langhorn and the pilot of the *Revenge*, both of whom were hopefully reported to be 'very rich', and 'a young gentleman who is neither a sailor nor a soldier' — a description which would seem to be that of Philip Gawdy. From Linschoten's description of a visit to *San Bernabe*, when she was later in Terceira, we learn that Bertendona had honoured his instructions and was treating his prisoners very well indeed. Linschoten was invited up to the stern gallery of the Spanish galleon and here found Bertendona dining with Captain Langhorn 'that sat by him and had on a suit of black velvet, but he could not tell us any thing for that he could speak no other language but English and Latin, which Bertendona also could a little speak'. The prisoners had freedom to go ashore and to carry their swords by their sides, a mark of great honour.

Philip Gawdy later wrote a letter to his brother which provides information on the conditions of his captivity in Lisbon. He had been asked to pay a very high ransom as he had been mistaken for a rich man, 'the son of the chief judge of London, or else of my Lord Mayor of London, or else of some other noble house'. But, while he tried to get his ransom lowered to a figure more suited to his real means, he had liberty of movement which 'was promised as the rest of our ship had'. Langhorn too was well received in Lisbon, 'and not any harm done unto him, but with good convoy sent to Setubal, and from thence unto England with all the rest of the Englishmen that were taken prisoners.'[19]

Sir Richard Grenville himself was borne with great care aboard *San Pablo* where Don Alonso 'used him humanely and condoled with him on his loss' and arranged for him to be cared for by his own surgeon. The stricken Englishman was much fêted in the Spanish flagship: 'The captains and gentlemen went to visit him, and to comfort him in his hard fortune, wondering at his courage and stout heart.' What Grenville made of all this admiration is unknown, for he spoke little or not at all as he weakened and at last died on the second or third day after the battle.[20]

The sources offer two choices of the dying hero's last words, both of which are probably apocryphal. Bertendona reported that he died saying 'as I know all that remains is a living death, it will be better to die,' no doubt suitable words to be read by the King. Linschoten tells us that he made his last speech in Spanish:

> Here die I Richard Grenville, with a joyful and quiet mind, for that I have ended my life as a true soldier ought to do, that hath fought for his country, Queen, religion and honour, whereby my soul most joyful departeth out of this body, and shall always leave behind it an everlasting fame of a valiant and true soldier that hath done his duty, as he was bound to do. But the others of my company have done as traitors and dogs, for which they shall be reproached all their lives and leave a shameful name for ever.[21]

It seems unlikely that a dying man could have made such a complex speech in an alien tongue, but these are the sort of words one might have expected Sir Richard Grenville to have said, especially the last sentence, which was deleted from early English translations of Linschoten as being too harsh a valediction. But Grenville was not a forgiving man and it seems suitable that with his last breath he should reproach and curse those shipmates who had denied him the honour of saving the *Revenge* from the hands of Spain.

CHAPTER FOURTEEN

THE DEVIL IN
THE SEA

Es menos riesgo pelear con ingleses
que con los tiempos.

There is less risk in fighting with the English
than with the weather.[1]

D ON ALONSO DE BAZÁN had obeyed the first part of his orders from
King Philip. He had sailed to the island of Flores and, once there,
had cleared the seas of English ships. It was now time to pay attention to
the main purpose of his voyage — to meet and escort home those treasure
fleets for which Lord Thomas Howard and Sir Richard Grenville had waited
so long in vain. Don Alonso ordered the armada to take up station west
of the islands and sent his *zabras* and caravels far out into the Atlantic to
search for the missing ships and shepherd them to the rendezvous. They
did not have to wait too long. On 7 September, a week after the battle,
eleven bedraggled and storm-tossed ships hove into sight. These were the
ships commanded by Antonio Navarro which had become separated from
the main body of the combined fleets some three weeks earlier. Don Alonso
heard the terrible story of their voyage and replenished them with water
and fresh provisions. His vigil then continued until daybreak six days later
when the forty-nine equally bedraggled ships under Aparicio de Arteaga
made contact with his scouts. By afternoon, they had joined the rest of
the armada and Don Alonso was able to discover the full extent of the
disasters experienced by the fleets. Nearly a quarter of the ships which
had left Havana had been lost in the continuous storms encountered
between Bermuda and the Azores and most of the survivors were in
a pitiable state. Masts, rigging and sails were damaged, stores ruined

by water, and crews and passengers were in the most wretched condition.[2]

The season was now well advanced and it would have been prudent to set sail for Spain as soon as possible. However, the King's orders had instructed the armada to escort home not just the treasure fleets, but also the frigates from Cartagena with their cargo of silver and gold and the long-expected fleet of Portuguese East-Indiamen from Goa. Don Alonso could hardly abandon such rich ships to the attention of Lord Thomas Howard's fleet or any English corsairs still lurking in the vicinity.

He called a *junta* to consider the matter. It was resolved that, despite the danger of the season, they should stay in the islands to await the frigates and East-Indiamen until 5 October at the latest, the deadline set by the King. The majority of the ships would proceed to Terceira to take on fresh supplies and repair some of the most badly damaged vessels, while the *zabras* and caravels stayed off Flores to watch out for Menendez and his frigates.[3]

On 15 September, the day after the *junta*, Don Alonso set sail for Terceira with a fleet of ninety-eight ships, sixty from the treasure fleets and the remainder from his own armada.[4] It was a fine morning and the good weather of the last few days seemed set to stay. But, by noon, there was an ominous darkening in the northern sky and the wind began to blow hard from the north-east. By dusk, it had shifted into the north and reached full gale force. As the sun sank into the sea, huge waves were rolling down against the fleet and the wind was lashing sails and rigging as the men clung on and tried to hold their course for Terceira.

The weather continued to deteriorate through the night and, in the feeble light of a dark dawn, Don Alonso could now see only ten ships from the huge fleet which had accompanied him into the night. One of these — the *Spíritu Santo* from San Domingo — soon sank at his side with only one survivor. All the other ships were so widely scattered that scarcely two of them were left together. For three days and nights, Don Alonso in *San Pablo* battled through horrendous seas, his foresail blown away and water pouring into his ship through gaping holes in her bows. The wind had now moved round into the west, driving him helplessly past the harbour at Angra where several anchored ships could be seen plunging wildly in the mountainous seas. At last, on the morning of 18 September, the weather moderated a little and he was able to come to anchor at Praia on the sheltered eastern side of Terceira. Divers went overboard to repair the bows of his galleon, while a messenger was sent overland to Angra to instruct the ships in the harbour to join him.

This was just a lull in a storm which left a lasting impression on all who witnessed it. 'Men who have grown old on the sea,' wrote Bazán, 'declare that they have never seen anything like it.' His words were echoed by Villavicencio who reported the storm as 'the greatest and longest lasting that I have ever seen and I heard very old sailors say the same'.[5] This, admittedly, is what Spaniards often said when they had endured a bad storm but, in this case, one feels that these men who had survived the tempests of Armada year were telling nothing less than the truth.

Falcão de Resende described how the storm appeared from the decks of *San Cristóbal de Portugal*:

A furious wind hurled itself upon our armada, destroying and dividing it, breaking masts and yards and sails and rigging, and weakening the strong bonds that held the ships together as it lashed at them with terrifying persistence. Extraordinary seas rose up which sought to engulf them, the waves now touching the heavens, now plummeting to the centre of the earth, filling the vessels with fear and water as one ship rose ever upwards to the summit of the wave and the next one plunged down, down into the trough.

Exhausted sailors struggled with the sails until at last the ships ran with bare masts before the wind, as the storm grew worse and worse.

So terrible and persistent [was it] that it became too much for human strength and no hope was left but to beseech the help of God and his saints. And so two horrendous nights and two sad and desolate days passed by and of our friends in other ships there were very few to be seen, scattered as they were by the black wings of the tempest.[6]

According to Linschoten, the storm looked no less fierce from the comparative security of Terceira:

> There suddenly rose so hard and cruel a storm, that those of the island did affirm that in man's memory there was never any such seen or heard of before: for it seemed the sea would have swallowed up the islands, the water mounting higher than the cliffs which are so high that it amazeth a man to behold them: but the sea reached above them and living fishes were thrown upon the land. This storm continued not only a day or two with one wind, but seven or eight days continually, the wind turning round about, in all places of the compass, at the least twice or thrice during that time, and all alike with a continual storm and tempest most terrible to behold, even to us that were on shore, much more then to such as were at sea.[7]

The men of Terceira who looked out on the black and terrible sea knew in their hearts what caused this storm to end all storms. This was God's punishment for the taking of the *Revenge*, a sure sign that 'hee took part with Lutherans and heretics.' Some went further and claimed the storm was the bitter revenge of that devil Sir Richard himself:

> So soon as they had thrown the dead body of the Vice-admiral Sir Richard Grenville over board, they verily thought that as he had a devilish faith and religion, and therefore ye devils loved him, so he presently sunk into the bottom of the sea, and down into Hell, where he raised up all the devils to the revenge of his death.[8]

Whether the crews in the ships shared such blasphemous and terrifying sentiments we do not know. Spanish and Portuguese sailors were certainly superstitious enough to believe almost anything as they battled with the elements. And battle they did, though not much could be done in such weather except to reduce sails to a minimum, put all spare men to the pumps, pray, and try desperately to steer a course that would avoid the islands between Flores and Terceira and then miss the coast of Terceira in its turn. Many failed. Ships piled up on São Jorge and Graciosa. Others were flung on to the south and west coasts of Terceira; on its north coast, the flagship of the Mexican fleet met its fate, one of the richest ships to be wrecked. Some ships were deliberately run aground to prevent them sinking or, like the *Santa Maria del Puerto*, abandoned as she began to sink 'less than two leagues from the harbour of Terceira'. Many of these ships had been rotting in the West Indies for months or even years and were in no condition to combat a cyclone, 'for the seas upon that coast engender a worm which does both weaken and consume their ships'.[9]

Don Alonso's respite from the storm did not last a single day. Barely had the repairs on *San Pablo* been started than the wind got up again and forced her off her temporary anchorage at Praia. The same wind blew nearly all the ships at Angra off their anchors. It scarcely seemed possible, but the seas now became even worse. The following day, St Michael's Day, was most terrible of all as huge winds and seas from the north-west crashed into the twenty or so ships in company with the flagship. A few ships were able to take shelter in São Miguel, but for the rest there was now only one hope left, to run under bare poles for Spain.

They raced on, masts and yards lost, rigging in tatters, pumps at full stretch, occasionally glimpsing through the waves and rain a sight of colleagues in distress or of wreckage from those for whom there was no longer hope. On St Michael's night, two galleons from the squadron of Castile collided 'with the great fury of the wind and the sea' and *San Medel* lost her beakhead and bowsprit 'without anyone being able to help'. Other ships were seen close to the Formigas, shoals which lay between Santa Maria and São Miguel — 'all those who hit them are lost.' Maldonado saw the flagship and *almiranta* (vice-admiral) of Urquiola's squadron fly by, together with the Apostle *Santo Tomás*, 'so badly damaged that there was little hope they would be able to resist the sea'. More ships from the treasure fleets were lost in this passage of the storm. 'On the island of St Michael [São Miguel],' wrote Linschoten, 'there were four ships cast away and between Terceira and St Michael's three more were sunk, which were seen and heard to cry out, whereof not one man saved.'

Amazingly, in the midst of this fury of the sea, English corsairs were taking advantage of the scattered Spanish ships. Captain Robert Flicke with the fleet of reinforcements from London had at last reached the Azores and, at the height of the storm on St Michael's Day, 'we fell among certaine of the Indian fleets which the said storme dispersed.' Two ships were forced to strike, although 'the seas were so growen, as neither with boat nor shippe they were to bee borded.' Later, it became a little calmer and they were able to offload some high-value, low-bulk goods, such as cochineal and silks, before both these prizes sank. A third prize, the *Nuestra Sēnora de los Remedios*, was also taken and brought safely back to Plymouth. Storm or not, this ship was boarded by the English sailors who broke into the chests of the Spanish crew and seized money and other valuables, much to Captain Flicke's disapproval. These English desperadoes did not have it all their own way. At the height of the tempest, Manuel Paez in the *Caçada*, one of Dom Luis's flyboats, fought a three-day running battle with one of the corsairs and managed to recapture a prize from the Englishmen.[10]

Don Alonso, continuing his course for Spain, knew nothing of these encounters, his pumps busy as the oakum packed into his bows was washed away and water began to flood in once again. The storm went on, day after day, night after night, the wind now blowing from the south-west with huge waves threatening to swallow up the sterns of the galleons, now swinging right round into the east so that their bows crashed into the endless seas with a shuddering, sickening impact as each wave was struck in turn. Nearly every ship had lost masts and spars. Many had several feet of water in their holds, but still they crashed and rolled on towards those seemingly unattainable havens on the Spanish and Portuguese mainland. If these two weeks of tempest were horrific for the sailors struggling on deck, they were worse still for the soldiers battened down below, soaked, sick, helpless and utterly terrified by the noise and ceaseless motion as their wooden prisons crashed from side to side and down into those abysmal troughs that seemed to descend for ever.

Then, at last, God heard their prayers, the storm gradually abated and ahead of them lay the hills of their homeland. The scattered fleet made many landfalls — Cadiz, San Lucar, Setubal, Oporto, Vigo, even as far north as Bayonne — but the largest group, including Don Alonso in *San Pablo*, made for Lisbon as the nearest place of safety. Falcão de Resende records the joy with which they saw the high rock of Cintra and the bar of the river Tagus, though ironically they were unable for some time to get into the river because of the lack of wind, 'whose excess had done so much damage so little time before'.

The first ships made port on 26 September, eleven days from the beginning of the storm. By 29 September, the great majority of those which would ever return had struggled in. At this point, it looked as though the losses would be truly terrible. Where were *Santiago de Portugal* and *San Bernardo*, last seen 'shattered on the islands and one had lost its foremast', or *San Medel*, glimpsed on the Formigas Shoals and given little hope? What had happened to *San Pedro*, last seen on St Michael's night in distress off the island of São Miguel? 'Many galleons are missing which were dismasted and damaged,' wrote Antonio Navarro. 'God preserve and bring them safe to port.' God did preserve all these and others which staggered back days later, many of the lost ships turning up at Vigo where Bertendona had managed to lead some six of the royal fleet home. He reckoned to have done the King a greater service in saving *San Bernabe* from the storm than in capturing the *Revenge*.[11]

How many ships were lost in this storm 'which lasted fourteen days'? English writers had a field day with this fresh manifestation of God's displeasure with Spain. Captain Monson said that 'nigh a hundred' of the ships in the treasure fleets were wrecked, 'from the time they met with the armada' — a splendid exaggeration since only sixty ships did meet with it. Sir Walter Raleigh got equally carried away, reporting fourteen wrecks on the island of São Miguel alone, 3,000 bodies on the shores of Terceira and altogether '10,000 cast away in this storm'. Linschoten reported twenty-six ships lost in the islands — seven on or near São Miguel, three on Graciosa, two on São Jorge, two on Pico and no fewer than twelve on Terceira:

and not only upon the one side, but round about it in every corner, whereby nothing else was heard but complaining, crying, lamenting, and telling here

> is a ship broken in pieces against the cliffs, and here another, and all the men drowned: so that for the space of twenty days after the storm, they did nothing else but fish for dead men that came continually driving on the shore.[12]

All these dramatic accounts are however grossly exaggerated. Many of these 'wrecks' either never happened at all or were cases where ships were in distress or ran ashore and were later recovered. The French historian Pierre Chaunu, who studied the registers recording the departures and arrivals of the Indies fleets, found only twenty ships lost and this number included those lost in the storms in mid-Atlantic as well as those lost in the islands.[13] He may have missed a few, but this figure seems to be about right. A careful scrutiny provides clear evidence of the shipwreck of just seven of the Indies fleets in the great storm which struck them in the islands, though others were so shattered that they never left Terceira and were later broken up. The rest either got home to Lisbon, San Lucar or Cadiz at the same time as the ships in the royal fleet, or managed to ride out the storm in the islands and then run the gauntlet of the English corsairs when the weather abated.

The losses in the royal fleet were also rather less dramatic than the fifteen or sixteen 'of the ships of war' claimed by Sir Walter Raleigh.[14] The *Madalena*, a privately owned ship in Urquiola's squadron, ran aground on Terceira after making a lot of water and was wrecked with the loss of half her crew, while the *petachio* from the same squadron simply vanished and was later discovered to have been lost on Graciosa. Another private man-of-war, the *Vegoña de Sevilla*, in Sancho Pardo's squadron sank in the open sea with the loss of 60 or 70 of her 200 men and one of Dom Luis Coutinho's flyboats was lost with all hands on the coast of Terceira. There may also have been another *petachio* wrecked, though the evidence is ambiguous. Many other ships from the royal fleet had very narrow escapes, but only these four, or possibly five, were actually wrecked in the islands. Two others were of course lost in the battle.

Even if the actual losses were far less than reported, this storm was a savage blow to the fine fleet which had left Ferrol with such pride and pomp just over two months previously. Six or seven ships had been lost completely and almost all the rest were in a terrible condition when they at last reached port. Four of the five Apostles which had sailed with the fleet were so badly damaged that they were unable to leave port for weeks; only *San Felipe* survived in sufficiently good shape to sail out of Lisbon on 12 October to escort the thirty merchant ships sheltered there and in Setubal to their planned destination in southern Spain. And only four galleons were declared 'fit enough' to accompany her. The rest were far too '*destrozados*', too shattered, to be risked again at sea until they had received extensive repairs, and when would that be done since there were no materials, no money and no skilled men to do the work? Well might Don Juan de Maldonado say, 'there is less risk fighting with the English than with the weather.'[15]

The sailors in King Philip's navy were normally men of few and blunt words when they made their reports, their quills only really taking flight when they were complaining. But when they wrote their letters to the King on this occasion, the strain and the emotion is evident. 'God's pity,' wrote Villavicencio as he described the ravaged state of the Apostle *Santo Tomás* when she reached Lisbon. 'God knows how we have managed,' wrote Urquiola. 'God knows what we have suffered!' wrote Aparicio de Arteaga. It seemed a high price to pay for the capture of one English galleon. 'The Spaniards make neither bonfires neither processions, but all very sad,' wrote Edmund Palmer from St Jean-de-Luz. And, in another letter, he reported that 'the Spaniards do not sing *Te Deums* about the streets neither make bonfires as they were wont of their victories, but are as still as a nest of young birds.'[16]

And where was the proof of that victory? Where was the one English galleon that had been so dearly won? The working party from Urquiola's squadron did a good job on the shattered galleon. By the time that Don Alonso set sail on 15 September, *La Venganza*, as she was now usually called by the Spaniards, had been fitted with new main and foremasts and was described by Maldonado as sailing very well. A crew of seventy men, including a few of the English prisoners, was put into her and her command was entrusted to the Basque Captain Landagorrieta.[17]

The *Revenge* may have sailed well as she departed from Flores, but she was soon in trouble once the storm struck the fleet. It looked as though Captain Langhorn would be correct in his prediction that 'with the first working of the sea, she must needs sink.' Don Alonso, fearful of the danger to his magnificent prize, ordered Marcos de Aramburu to go with his squadron to the *Revenge* and try to effect further repairs if the weather moderated. The continuing fury of the storm prevented this, but Aramburu kept close to the prize, as did Don Martín de Bertendona in *San Bernabe*. But, alas, so dreadful was the storm that the efforts of these shepherds were in vain and the Spaniards were denied the honour of sailing into the Tagus with the finest galleon in the world.

Linschoten records:

> Among the rest was the English ship called the *Revenge*, that was cast away upon a cliff near to the island of Terceira, where it brake in a hundred pieces and sunk to the ground, having in her 70 men, gallegos, Biscaines, and others, with some of the captive Englishmen, whereof but one was saved that got up upon the cliffs alive, and had his body and head all wounded, and he being on shore brought us the news, desiring to be shriven, and thereupon presently died.

The *Revenge* had made her last voyage. Don Alonso did not hear this sad news until he arrived in Lisbon. His report of the loss of the prize shows genuine emotion. 'I have felt this very deeply,' he wrote to the King, 'for she was such a noble ship and carried such fine artillery.' No other ship wrecked in the storm earned such an epitaph.[18]

Where did the *Revenge* sink? Many people have asked this question and their speculations nearly always begin and end with Linschoten's graphic description of the *Revenge* 'cast away upon a cliff near to the island of Terceira'. Almost anyone who reads this and then visits Terceira will be certain that only in one place is there a cliff 'near to' rather than on the island. This is on the two huge rocks called the Ilhéus das Cabras (the Islands of the She-goats) which stand up prominently in the sea about a thousand yards off the south coast of the island. Much time and effort has been spent by divers in swimming round these rocks looking for the guns of the *Revenge* in order to return them to their rightful resting place in the Tower of London, as one team put it.

Such patriotic endeavour would have been better served if it had been backed by rather more research. This would have led to the discovery of a letter written on 14 October 1591 from Terceira by Captain Suarez de Salazar who had replaced Juan de Horbina as Governor of the Azores. His letter states fairly precisely where the wreck of the *Revenge* lay: 'The *almiranta* in which came Ricarte de Campo Verde, after Your Majesty's fleet had taken it, was lost on this island in a very rugged place which they call La Serreta.'[19] This description almost certainly refers to the coastline which falls away very steeply below the sloping fields of the village of Serreta in the north-west of the island. Such a site for the wreck makes good sense, since this is the first place that a ship might be expected to strike if it took a direct line from Flores to Terceira. This part of Terceira is indeed very rugged (*'asperissimo'*). The view to the south along the coast of Serreta from Ponta do Queimado is one of the wildest stretches of rugged cliffs and rocks that one could imagine. It seems a suitable graveyard for the *Revenge*.

Both Linschoten and Suarez de Salazar noted in their accounts that the islanders thought it would be possible to salvage the guns of the wrecked galleon. 'The *Revenge* had in her divers fair brass peeces that were all sunk in the sea, which they of the island were in good hope to weigh up again,' wrote Linschoten. 'I am informed they can salvage [the guns] at some cost,' reported the governor to the King. His letter was endorsed in Spain: 'This will be very good; see that the guns are salvaged with much care.'[20]

Things generally happened very slowly in the Spanish Empire, but it seems that the twenty-two remaining guns of the *Revenge* were eventually salvaged and that her magnificent lower-deck battery no longer lies on the bottom of the sea to await an inquisitive diver. The first clue comes in September 1603 when Captain Pedro de Lumbieras, an artillery officer in the garrison of Terceira, wrote a letter to the King which was discussed in the Council of War in the following year. Lumbieras referred to the guns of the *Revenge* and then said that 'in the years 1592 and 1593 they salvaged fourteen pieces from her, leaving six or seven that they could not get at very well and that now [i.e. in 1603 — ten years later] storms have dragged them closer to the coast so that they could easily be salvaged.' He had reported this to the captain-general of artillery in Terceira, but was told no money could be spared to do the work. The Council of War recommended that 500 ducats be paid to enable these remaining guns to be salvaged, 'and as soon as possible since we know that the said guns were very good and there is such a shortage of artillery on the island.'[21] This is a remarkable testimony to the quality of the guns of the *Revenge*, still thought worth salvaging at considerable cost after thirteen years in the sea.

Over twenty years later, the guns had still not been forgotten as salvage had turned out to be less easy than predicted by Lumbieras. There were still two left in the sea, 'which were very difficult to salvage'. Don Pedro Estevan d'Avila, captain of the fortress of San Phelipe in Angra, informed the King that

> in the part of this island where the English *almiranta* of Ricardo de Campo Verde ran aground, they have salvaged some of the best bronze guns which we have in this castle. The salvor is a gunner called Sebastiano Rivero ... He has now offerred to salvage two that are still under her side and deliver them to the gate of this city, on condition that we pay him 100 *escudos* for each gun on account of his salary.

Rivero was no doubt used to such bargaining since we learn from another letter that he had already salvaged eighteen bronze guns from the *Revenge*, a number that implies that he not only salvaged the guns recovered in 1603, but also most of those recovered in 1592 and 1593. He must have been a remarkable man who would have been at least fifty when he set off for La Serreta to salvage the last two guns of the *Revenge*, nearly thirty-four years after she was wrecked.[22] We only know for certain that he salvaged one of them. On 4 July 1625, d'Avila reported that he had accepted Rivero's offer and 'today he has brought me a bronze demi-cannon of about 40 quintals weight which I have put in the castle . . . paying him 100 *escudos* for this gun on account of his salary.' D'Avila begged the King to reward the salvor with a bonus, since he was not only a good diver but also a very good gunner.[23]

One feels sufficient confidence in the ability of Sebastiano Rivero to be certain that he did manage to recover the last remaining gun of the *Revenge*, however difficult it may have been. It was unsung heroes like him, often unpaid for months or even years, who kept the far-flung Spanish Empire going. How he managed to salvage a forty-quintal (two-ton) gun from underneath the wreck we do not know. However, there is no doubt that he did, with no breathing apparatus and no modern lifting equipment. It was a remarkable achievement and he certainly deserved a bonus.

And so the guns of the *Revenge* will never find a home in the armoury of the Tower of London. 'The finest artillery which has ever been seen in a sailing ship' does not lie on the bottom of the sea awaiting discovery by a twentieth-century scuba diver. It was recovered long ago and no doubt has long since been melted down for scrap. But it is good to report that, for many many years before that happened, these masterpieces of the art of the Elizabethan gun-founder were considered to be some of the finest guns that graced that lonely bastion in the middle of the Atlantic, the castle of San Phelipe in Terceira.

CHAPTER FIFTEEN

AN HEROICAL FABLE

Yet shall thy deeds outlive the day of doome
For even Angels in the heavens shall sing
Grenville unconquered died, still conquering.[1]

E VEN AFTER 400 YEARS, the last fight of the *Revenge* is still a good
story and worth retelling with the benefit of research in the Spanish
archives. None the less, readers might be forgiven for wondering why this
one incident in the long Elizabethan war against Spain became so famous
and why the memory of it has endured so long. It was after all an English
defeat and it had no strategic significance in the conduct of the war. The
English are of course well known for glamorizing their defeats and their
retreats, as the stories of Corunna, Dunkirk and the charge of the Light
Brigade bear witness. The last fight of the *Revenge* was also marvellous, but
is that enough to account for its enduring fame?

One explanation for the continuing attraction of the story was suggested
by the naval historian, David Hannay, in 1904. 'The Elizabethan epic would
want its most purple patch if there had been no fight at Flores in the Azores,'
he wrote and this may be read as meaning that, if there had been no last fight
of the *Revenge*, it would have been necessary to invent one.[2] The Elizabethan
epic has many facets, but one is certainly heroism at sea. And yet there is no
great naval battle to provide a focus for admiration, hero worship and glory.
The defeat of the Armada does not quite fill the bill, since it was the result
not of a bloody and heroic battle but the product of a variety of factors, such
as the miscalculations of the Spanish commanders and the savage storms
which struck their fleet. If there had been a Nelson and a Trafalgar in the
Elizabethan period, we would have heard less about Sir Richard Grenville.
But there was not and so his magnificent but ultimately pointless defence of
his ship and the indomitable courage of her fighting men became the focus
of English pride.

A simple story does not become a 'purple patch' without the attention of a master of propaganda and in 1591 there was one ready at hand in the person of Sir Walter Raleigh, who deliberately set out to make the fight famous only a few weeks after the event.[3] Partly as a memorial to his kinsman and friend, Sir Richard Grenville, but mainly as a piece of brilliant propaganda against Spain, Raleigh penned his first published pamphlet — 'A report of the trueth of the fight about the Isles of Açores, the last of August 1591 betwixt the Revenge, one of her Majesties shippes, and an Armada of the King of Spaine'. The odds are thus set out in the title and the pamphlet goes on to compare the empty bombast of vainglorious and over-mighty Spain with the astonishing achievements of small numbers of gallant Englishmen. Raleigh starts with a brief account of the defeat of the Armada, 'which they termed invincible, consisting of 140 saile', but was 'by 30 of her Majesties owne ships of war, and a few of our owne Marchants . . . beaten and shuffled together'. He then gives a short, but very flattering, account of the Portugal expedition of 1589, when 'a handfull of souldiers' achieved so much, before going on to the story of the last fight of the *Revenge*.

Here, as elsewhere in the pamphlet, Raleigh exaggerated, though not so obviously as to undermine his thesis that English valour would always be a match for great multitudes of foreigners — a belief that was to become self-evident truth for Englishmen in the centuries that followed. Raleigh thus gave the right number of Spanish ships in Bazán's armada, but grossly augmented their numbers of guns and soldiers while the size, armament and crew of the *Revenge* were minimized. No one doubts that the *Revenge* fought against great odds, but they were not quite the odds described by Raleigh and accepted uncritically by all historians until quite recently.

The description of the fight itself is a fine piece of Elizabethan prose which can stir the blood today just as it was meant to in 1591, but once again Raleigh overstated his case; fifteen Spanish ships fought alongside the *Revenge* or boarded her instead of five, all the gunpowder was expended, the last pike broken, and so on. Every effort was thus made to inflate a fight which was astonishing enough in all truth into a struggle of truly mythical proportions. So powerful and successful was Raleigh's pen that Grenville had already entered the pantheon of English heroes and his last fight had become a legend before Christmas of the year in which it had been fought. The contemporary Spanish historian, Cabrera de Córdoba, was to write a well-balanced account of the battle, based on the official Spanish *relación* and giving due credit to the English defence, but it was too late. Even Spaniards believed Raleigh's hyperbole while no English writer seems to have used Cabrera de Córdoba's account until now.[4]

Raleigh set a tone for describing the battle which was soon followed by others. Gervase Markham headed the field with 'The Most Honourable Tragedie of Sir Richard Grinvile Knight', an epic poem written in 1595 which was described with delightful irony by its nineteenth-century editor: 'Whatever may be its merits, it does certainly help us to realize the long duration of the battle.'[5] The merits are few, but the poem certainly takes the 'mangled carkasse but unmaimed minde' of Sir Richard Grenville one step further into the realms of glory. Where Raleigh and then Markham had led, others were soon to follow, mercifully at shorter length than the execrable Markham.

Sir Richard Hawkins in his *Observations* of 1622 thought the fight might 'worthily be written in our Chronicles in letter of Gold, in memory for all posterities, some to beware, and others by their example in the like occasions to imitate the true valour of our Nation in those Ages'. These two themes — the warning to foreigners to beware the fighting Englishman and the encouragement to each new generation to learn the story and to emulate it — were to be regular keynotes in the literary references to Grenville. The story could also be used in the service of policy as Sir Francis Bacon demonstrated a few years later, when he penned a pamphlet advocating a war against Spain.

In this, he wondered why, in fights between Englishmen and Spaniards, 'the English, upon all encounters, have perpetually come off with honour, and the better.' He concluded that it was a result of the 'naturall courage of the people'. His prime example of this courage was Grenville's last fight which was memorable (I say) even beyond credit, and to the height of some heroical fable. And though it were a defeat yet it exceeded a Victory; being like the act of Samson, that killed more men at his death than he had done in the time of all his life.

Half a century later, John Evelyn wrote a history of commerce and navigation in which he included a discussion of England's mastery at sea. Once again, Grenville and the *Revenge* were singled out for praise and admiration. 'Than this what have we more! What can be greater!'[6] The story had by-passed history and entered legend, while Grenville had become the symbol of the indomitable Englishman who would fight all comers until death or victory. Foreigners beware!

Though dominant, this theme of English valour and heroism in the face of terrible odds was paralleled by a more critical undercurrent of writing which, far from seeing Grenville as a true hero, regarded him as a foolish, wilful man who by his own vainglory had lost the Queen one of her finest ships. Raleigh himself had gently criticized the conduct of his cousin in attempting to break through the Spanish squadrons: 'The other course had been the better.' Two other writers were to be far more severe on Grenville. The most influential was Sir William Monson who was much respected for his knowledge of naval affairs. His brief account of the battle was probably based on discussions with survivors whom he met while a captive in Lisbon, though he did not write it down until some thirty years after the event. Monson described Grenville as headstrong and rash and he has no word of praise for the courage of Sir Richard and his men. The *Revenge* was taken 'by the unadvised negligence and wilful obstinacy of the captain, Sir Richard Greynvile'. Monson's criticisms were similar to those of Sir Arthur Gorges, a pedantic writer who in 1597 had described Grenville as 'a man very wilfull and violent in his courses'.[7]

Both these writers also implied that Grenville was disobedient as well as wilful. Gorges, for instance, wrote that Grenville 'could in no wise be perswaded to follow his Admirall and his consorts. But thrusting himselfe rashly in amongst the Spaniards . . . ' Linschoten is even more specific on this point: 'But when they perceyved the Kings Army [i.e. armada] to be strong, the Admirall being the Lorde Thomas Howard commaunded his Fleete not to fall upon them . . . notwithstanding the Vice Admirall Sir Richard Greenfield . . . went into the Spanish fleete, and shot among them.' More recent naval historians have made great play with this accusation of disobedience — Sir John Laughton for instance claiming that the true moral of the fight was 'the disastrous effect of disobedience'.[8] Others have used the incident to compare Grenville with Nelson and to speculate on when it is the duty of a captain to turn a blind eye to orders.

There is however no real evidence that Grenville actually was disobedient. Lord Thomas Howard did not perceive 'the King's army to be strong' until he was well clear of the anchorage. It is difficult to see how he could then have given such an order to Sir Richard Grenville, who was so far in his rear, in the absence of a much more sophisticated system of naval signalling than currently existed. As it was, Sir Richard may have been guilty of negligence in leaving the anchorage so slowly but, once he got to sea, he made every effort to obey the last order he had received — 'to follow his Admirall and his consorts'.

The image of Grenville which was carried into the great period of English naval warfare between 1650 and 1815 was thus rather a mixed one, neatly summed up by his entry in the mid-eighteenth-century *Biographia Britannica*: 'In the opinion of most, his memory merits immortal praise: yet others consider him as a martyr to his own obstinacy, and one who sacrificed the Queen's ship and subjects to that fantastic appearance of honour which so often misleads heroes.'[9] Such dualism in the estimation of Grenville was to continue into our own time. But, obstinate or not, Grenville was to remain one of the most famous of England's fighting sailors and his last fight provided a yardstick by which the courage and determination of lesser sailors could be judged. It was an awkward yardstick for the faint-hearted.

Each generation re-creates its heroes to suit the age and the reputation of Grenville was to undergo a sea-change in Victorian times. He now reached the apogee of his fame, but became in the process a rather different person from the one presented in this book. The first signs of reassessment come in an article published by the historian J.A. Froude in the *Westminster Review* of July 1852. This essay on the great Elizabethan seamen was crowned by a description of the last fight of the *Revenge*. 'We shall close,' he wrote:

> amidst the roar of cannon, and the wrath and rage of battle ... At the
> time all England and all the world rang with it. It struck a deeper terror,
> though it was but the action of a single ship, into the hearts of the Spanish
> people — it dealt a more deadly blow upon their fame and moral strength,
> than the destruction of the Armada itself.

The man who struck this terror into the hearts of his enemies 'was a goodly
and gallant gentleman, who had never turned his back upon an enemy, and
remarkable in that remarkable time for his constancy and daring'.[10]

This goodly and gallant image was further developed by Charles Kingsley
in his popular *Westward Ho!*, first published during the Crimean War in 1855,
a time when England might well feel the need of heroes from her past.
Kingsley's book was written in memory of the Elizabethan mariners, 'their
voyages and their battles, their faith and their valour, their heroic lives and
no less heroic deaths'. Most heroic of all was Sir Richard Grenville who now
took on the character of a brave Victorian gentleman, 'wise and gallant ...
lovely to all good men, awful to all bad men; in whose presence none dare
say or do a mean or a ribald thing' — not the sort of chap who burned
down churches, even papist ones.[11]

Kingsley's image stuck, but it was Tennyson who set the seal on
the Elizabethan hero's national fame. 'The Revenge: a ballad of the fleet'
appeared in the March 1878 number of *Nineteenth Century*, at the peak of
Britain's world power, and the poem struck an immediate chord with the
British people.[12] Tennyson followed Raleigh closely for the bare fabric of
the story, which he then so effectively embroidered. His sonorous, stirring
verses were even more memorable than Raleigh's stately prose, fortunately
for those generations of schoolchildren who had to learn the poem by heart:

> I have fought for Queen and Faith
>   like a valiant man and true;
> I have only done my duty
>   as a man is bound to do.

The public loved it and, by 1900, the last fight of the *Revenge* was even better known and even more admired than it had been in 1600.

Such bravery and steadfastness were an object lesson for empire-builders and, as such, a good subject for the writers of stories for boys as Robert Leighton among others realized. In *The Golden Galleon* of 1898, the last fight of the *Revenge* comes as a fitting climax to the adventures of two young lads from Devon, Master Gilbert Oglander and his squire Timothy Trollope, the valiant son of a Plymouth barber. In his introduction, Leighton wrote that the worst that could be said of Grenville's exploit was 'that it was the Balaclava charge of the Spanish war; at its best it was an example, and a very grand example, of that British pluck and intrepidity which have ever been the distinguishing characteristics of our fighting countrymen.' There is plenty of British pluck in the book but, dominating all, is the character of Sir Richard Grenville whose voice

> seemed to have in it something of the deep roar of the sea waves breaking upon cavernous rocks. He was a very excellent gentleman, a loyal subject of the Queen, and a very proper Christian. In an age when cruelty in war was common he fought with a truly British sense of fairness.[13]

Boys may have been convinced by this image, but some men were still not quite sure. The period from about 1890 to 1930 was a great one for Tudor naval history. Writers such as Laughton, Corbett, Hannay, Oppenheim, Williamson and Callender reinterpreted the origins of English maritime power in the light of contemporary conceptions of naval strategy and tactics. These historians focused their attention on Drake and Hawkins, on the defeat of the Spanish Armada and, above all, on a search for the origins of the modern in the Elizabethan past. They were especially interested in the development of big guns and the concept of a naval battle as an artillery duel. Close fights, boarding and hand-to-hand combat were seen as anachronisms, ways of fighting at sea which Spaniards might be expected to adopt, but not Englishmen. Grenville's last fight fits uneasily into such an analysis and was treated with a mixture of admiration of his courage, censure of his rashness and supposed disobedience and a certain embarrassment that an

Englishman could behave in such a wilful and self-destructive way, 'an act of madness redeemed by valour' as David Hannay put it.[14]

This historical dilemma was resolved by praising Grenville, but distancing him from his respectable contemporaries, like Hawkins, who carried out naval warfare in the way thought proper by such historians. Grenville's action was thus compared with the feats of the heroes of the far-distant past, with Leonidas and his 300 Spartans at Thermopylae, with the Chevalier Bayard, the true stuff of legend.[15] Grenville himself was sometimes seen as a man of the Renaissance: 'He thought a great deal of triumphing superbly, and of dying in a blaze of glory, leaving behind him that reputation which the Renaissance world cherished as a species of prolongation of life.' He and his men were the victims of his noble blood from which he inherited 'the firm conviction that it was his right to sacrifice the lives of his followers if he could thereby earn honour for himself and his house. Their honour was to die with their lord.'[16]

Grenville was more often portrayed by contrast as a medieval throwback, a representative of a class of Elizabethan Englishmen who, in Sir Julian Corbett's words, 'had in it more of the fabled knight-errantry of the Middle Ages than of the naval science ... of Tudor times, men whose restless passion for adventure was turned, as in the days of their crusading ancestors, into a war for the religion they so ardently professed and as ruthlessly transgressed.'[17] Some writers threw Grenville back even further. David Hannay, for instance, thought that Grenville's action would have been 'understood by a generation that revelled in Marlowe and knew what was meant by an "heroic fury"', a fury driven in his case by the Norse blood in his gentle Devonian veins. This image was repeated by J. B. Black in his *Reign of Elizabeth* when he described the last fight as 'this remarkable display of berserker valour', an adjective which describes the frenzied fury of wild Norse warriors on the battlefield.[18]

While such writers were careful to distance themselves from Grenville's fury, indiscipline and anachronism, they and others were also quick to point up the useful lessons for the naval tradition. Good fighters and instinctive courage were still needed by the ironclad navy just as they had been in the past. Robert Louis Stevenson, in his essay on the English admirals, thought the story 'mad', but felt that such mad stories were necessary 'not only to enliven men of the sword as they go into battle, but [also to] send back merchant clerks with more heart and spirit to their book-keeping by double entry'. Sir Julian Corbett believed that any sailor untouched by the Grenville spirit was 'unfit to command a ship-of-war', a daunting challenge to his naval contemporaries. Gerard Fiennes also recognized the demonstrative value of the last fight of the *Revenge* when he wrote *Sea Power and Freedom* in the middle of the First World War:

> Grenville's exploit and his end warmed the courage of the men of his own day, and have warmed the courage of British seamen ever since. A country cannot afford to look coldly on such great fights against odds if it would see the martial spirit of its sons maintained.[19]

Raleigh's spirited propaganda has clearly had its effect. The last fight of the *Revenge* is not likely to be forgotten, even if it is rather less well known today than in the more martial England of some forty or fifty years ago when a naval tradition begun in Grenville's time was still the backbone of the country's pride. The story has been retold here in the spirit of my own age, using Spanish sources to give the Spanish point of view and honouring the humble as well as their commanders. Courage and martial glory are often belittled in our post-imperial age, though England still wants heroes as press coverage of recent wars bears witness. Sir Richard Grenville was such a hero, even if readers may find it difficult to sympathize with his vainglory and his suicidal disregard for the lives of his men. Many may well decide that it was these men who were the true heroes, this 'tag and rag' who were prepared 'to spend their lives and limbs in this service for the good of our native country of England'.[20]

NOTES

ABBREVIATIONS

Add.	Additional
AGS	Archivo General de Simancas
APC	*Acts of the Privy Council*
Bertendona	D. Martín de Bertendona to S.M., Vigo, 8 October 1591 [AGS GA 326/61 & other copies] translated in E.M. Tenison, *Elizabethan England* (Leamington Spa, 1933–60) viii, 469–72
BL	British Library
CM2aE	Contaduria Mayor: segunda época, AGS
CSPD	*Calendar of State Papers, Domestic*
CSPSp	*Calendar of State Papers, Spanish*
Estado	Estado, AGS
Falcão de Resende	Andrés Falcão de Resende, *Romance do succeso da armada que foi as Ilhas Terceiras no anno de 1591* in C. Fernández Duro, *La Conquista de las Azores en 1583* (Madrid, 1866) pp. 133–48
GA	Guerra Antigua, AGS
HCA	High Court of Admiralty
HMC	Historical Manuscripts Commission
MM	*Mariner's Mirror*
NRS	Navy Records Society
PRO	Public Record Office
Raleigh	Sir Walter Raleigh, *A Report of the Truth of the Fight about the Isles of Açores* (1591) in Richard Hakluyt, *Principal Navigations* (Glasgow, 1903–5) vii, 38–53
Relación	Relación de lo sucedido a la armada de su magestad sobre la ysla de Flores en 9 de setiembre 1591 [AGS GA 341/331 & other copies] transcribed and translated in E. M. Tenison, *Elizabethan England* (Leamington Spa, 1933–60) viii, 484 a–f
SP	State Papers
Tennyson	Alfred Tennyson, 'The Revenge: a ballad of the fleet' (1878) in *Poems and Plays*, ed. Warren (Oxford, 1971)
WO	War Office

The notes normally refer only to the surname of the author, or the first word or words of the titles of anonymous works, and the date of publication. For full details of references, see the Bibliography (pp. 184). For abbreviations see above.

CHAPTER ONE

1 *Documentos* (1916) iv, 59.
2 Tenison (1933–60) vii, 360. See also Strong (1977), chapters 4 & 5.
3 Strong (1977) p. 121; Williams (1975) pp. 183–6.
4 There are many histories of the Armada, but this passage relies mainly on the recent books by Rodriguez Salgado (1988), Martin & Parker (1988) (quotations taken from pp. 236, 257) and Fernández-Armesto (1988) (quotation from p. 217).
5 *Documentos* (1916) iv, 56.
6 Martin & Parker (1988) p. 258; Camden (1688) p. 418.
7 *Documentos* (1916) iv, 56, 61; Speed (1688) p. 862.
8 See the analysis by Strong (1977) p. 43.

9   For the navy in 1590 see the list in Anderson (1957).
10 Quoted by Waters (1975) p. 4.
11 The relative number and quality of Spanish and English guns have been the subject
    of considerable debate which now seems to have been resolved. For Spanish guns see
    Thompson (1975) and, for the English guns, Lewis (1961), though Lewis's exaggeration
    of Spanish firepower makes his conclusions no longer tenable. For a useful discussion of
    this subject see Martin & Parker (1988).
12 Bacon (1629) pp. 52–3; PRO SP 94/4 fos. 64v & 71.

CHAPTER TWO

1   Raleigh (1829) viii, 325.
2   Quoted by Wernham (1984) p. 3. This book is the main authority for the discussion
    of strategy and foreign policy in this chapter.
3   On the Portugal expedition see Wernham (1984) chs. 5 & 6 and Wernham (1988).
4   AGS Estado 167. Molina to SM, Santander, 5/15 June 1589.
5   Williamson (1927) pp. 450–2.
6   In the summer of 1589, the Earl of Cumberland sailed with three privateers of his
    own and one Queen's ship to the Azores and, in September of the same year, Sir Martin
    Frobisher led a small fleet to lie off Cape St Vincent. These two fleets were back home
    by the end of the year and, mainly because of invasion scares, it was not until May 1590
    that six ships under Sir John Hawkins sailed to lie off Cape Finisterre and watch Ferrol.
    Another six ships under the command of Frobisher sailed to the Azores where they did
    not arrive until August.

CHAPTER THREE

1   Tennyson.
2   Williamson (1927) p. 387.
3   Bushnell (1936); Rowse (1937). These two books rely quite heavily on a well-researched
    article by Chope (1917) and these three works are the main authorities for this biographical
    sketch of Grenville.
4   George Granville, later Lord Lansdowne, 1710, quoted by Rowse (1937) p. 15.
5   *Biographia* (1750–7) p. 2283.
6   Rowse (1937) pp. 54–5.
7   Quoted by Rowse (1937) p. 137.
8   Quoted by Bushnell (1936) p. 75.
9   *CSPSp* ii, 481.
10 Quoted by Chope (1917) pp. 216–17.
11 Quinn (1955) i, 174. This work is the main authority on the Virginia voyages.
12 Quoted by Rowse (1937) p. 216. See also Fernández de Navarrete xxv, No. 53.
13 Quoted by Quinn (1955) i, 480; see also ii, 792 for the relation of Pedro Diaz.
14 Fernández de Navarrete xxv, No. 53, p. 408, translated by Rowse (1937) p. 220.
15 AGS GA 326/61, Bertendona to King, Vigo, 8 October 1591; Lane in Quinn (1955) i, 212.
16 Quoted by Quinn (1955) i, 192–3. Quinn supports this story, suggesting that Grenville
    had probably left his ship's boats for the use of the colonists. Fernández de Navarrete
    (1971) xxv, p. 405.
17 Linschoten (1598) p. 193.
18 AGS GA 326/36; GA 341/331; Hakluyt (1903–5) iv, 247; Linschoten (1598) p.
    193.
19 *CSPSp.* iii, 93, 110.

CHAPTER FOUR

1   Quoted by Waters (1975) p. 4.

2 John Stanhope to the Earl of Shrewsbury, Greenwich, 10 March 1590/91 in Lodge (1791) iii, 28.
3 Callender (1919) p. 95; Corbett (1899) i, 350; AGS GA 326/36; 326/61.
4 Hakluyt (1903–5) iv, 225. This description of the Revenge relies mainly on Oppenheim (1896), Glasgow (1966), Salisbury (1966), Smith (1970), Waters (1975), Howard (1979) and Kirsch (1990).
5 Hakluyt (1903–5) vi, 415.
6 Quoted by Oppenheim (1896) p. 127.
7 PRO SP12/239/21.
8 AGS GA 326/36.
9 This description of the guns draws on Lewis (1961); Martin & Parker (1988) and on the Spanish descriptions in relación pp. 484–5; AGS GA 326/26 & 341/198.
10 Martin & Parker (1988) p. 53.
11 For the delivery of gunpowder and small arms see PRO SP/12/238/51. The five royal ships had a total tonnage of 1,860 (see page 53) of which the Revenge provided 500 or 26.9 per cent. A last of gunpowder weighed 24 hundredweight, each hundredweight being 112 pounds of which 12 pounds was the weight of the cask and 100 pounds the gunpowder. Bourne (1587) p. 72.
12 References to Tennyson are to his poem, 'The Revenge: a ballad of the fleet'. The generalization about ages is derived from a quick analysis of the ages of deponents in PRO HCA 13.
13 Raleigh's accounts in PRO SP12/238/164. In all the pre-voyage calculations, the Revenge is reckoned as having 250 men, but Sir Richard Hawkins [Hawkins (1933) p. 16] said there were 'about two hundreth and sixtie men, as by the pay-booke appeareth', so this is presumably accurate.
14 PRO SP12/238/164; HMC Hatfield MSS iv, 119–20.
15 Hawkins (1933) p. 28; Raleigh (1829) viii, 346–7.
16 For Langhorn see Gawdy (1906) pp. 53, 56, 61 and Monson (1902–14) i, 259. Elizabethan ships normally carried soldiers as one-third of their numbers, though there is some doubt whether the ships of Lord Thomas Howard's fleet did. Two men who saw the English fleet leave London and later reported to the Spanish authorities both said there were only sailors and no soldiers ['va en ella ningun soldado']. AGS GA 341/293, relación of Antonio de Sousa; GA 341/294, relación of 'un maestre flamenco'. Raleigh also says that there were no soldiers in the Revenge. [Raleigh p. 43] On the other hand, Langhorn is described as captain of the soldiers by Monson (1902–14) i, 259.
17 Andrews (1982) p. 246.
18 Pay scales for 1582 from Corbett (1898) pp. 259–60.
19 Gawdy (1906) pp. 53–4.

CHAPTER FIVE

1 Sir John Hawkins's orders for the voyage of the Jesus of Lubeck in 1564. Hakluyt (1903–5) x, 10.
2 Smith (1970) p. 48 — bonnets and drablers were pieces of canvas laced to the bottom of sails to extend them. Gawdy (1906) pp. 58–9.
3 Gawdy (1906) p. 56; Smith (1970) p. 50.
4 Details on sailing etc. from Kirsch (1990) and Harland (1984).
5 Gawdy (1906) p. 54; Andrews (1964) — details of privateering ships on pp. 243–64.
6 For these voyages see Foster (1940); Williams (1975) pp. 207–9; Andrews (1959) pp. 95–172; Andrews (1964) pp. 164–7; 214–15; Williamson (1920) pp. 70–82. Cumberland quote from Stone (1965) p. 365.
7 Andrews (1959) pp. 167–72.
8 Date of departure and rumours can be found in Spanish reports of information collected in English waters. AGS GA 341/291-94. The date of departure is given as 5 April in Howard v. Watts [Andrews (1959) p. 169] and 3/13 April in Spanish sources.

9 BL Lansdowne 70 fos. 229v–230.
10 Gawdy (1906) p. 57; on events in Falmouth see AGS GA 341/291 and Andrews (1959) p. 171. 'Fishes' were supports of wood used as splints to strengthen a cracked mast or yard. 'Wolding' was a method of tightening a rope by winding round and round with a hand-spike, the same word being used for a horrible torture practised by pirates and privateers in which a rope was tightened round the victim's forehead until his eyes burst out.
11 Gawdy (1906) pp. 57–8. BL Lansdowne 67 fos. 150, 190. For later disputes over the prize see PRO SP12/242/42. On the Burlings see Monson (1902–14) ii, 254.
12 Shilton & Holworthy (1932) p. 18.
13 Gawdy (1906) pp. 59–63.
14 Corbett (1905) p. 36; Smith (1970) pp. 48–9.
15 Quoted by Keevil (1957) i, 80.
16 In fact, such descriptions may well be exaggerated. See the discussion of naval discipline during the Seven Years War in Rodger (1986).
17 Ambiguous and often conflicting information on discipline can be found in such works as Oppenheim (1896), Monson (1902–14), Corbett (1905), Boteler (1929), Smith (1970).
18 Wright (1951) pp. lxxx–lxxxi; Gawdy (1906) p. 58.
19 On the *Madre de Deus* see Kingsford (1912); Williamson (1920) pp. 83–112 and documents in BL Lansdowne 70 and PRO SP12/243–4.
20 *APC* 13 June 1591; Fernández de Navarrete (1971) xxv, No. 53; PRO HCA 13/28 f. 146v.
21 Hakluyt (1903–5) iv, 242; vii, 113, 118; Monson (1902–14) iv, 83; Gawdy (1906) pp. 61–2.
22 Idem p. 61 for the caravel. BL Lansdowne 67 fo. 172v & AGS GA 323/1 for *La Concepción*.

CHAPTER SIX

1 Sir Roger Williams, quoted in Wernham (1969) p. 467.
2 Lockhart & Otte (1976) pp. 117–19.
3 Ibid. pp. 85–6. Silver production in Hamilton (1934) p. 34.
4 On the fleet system in general see Haring (1918) and for the year-by-year details see Chaunu (1955).
5 On the defence of the Indies see Hussey (1929) and Hoffman (1980).
6 BL Lansdowne 67 f. 155; see also Chaunu (1955) iii, 458, fn. 6, for reluctance to load silver on the *fregatas*.
7 Wright (1951) pp. 226–7. This section on shipping in Havana relies mainly on this book, pp. lxxv–lxxxv & 256–80, and on Chaunu (1955) iii, 450–84.
8 Wright (1951) p. 258.
9 For details of the corsairs see Andrews (1959) pp. 95–107.
10 This account of the fight of the *Content* rests mainly on the description by her master, William King of Ratcliffe, which is printed in Andrews (1959) pp. 107–12. Other details can be found in Ibid pp. 154, 158, 164, 166 and in Wright (1951) pp. 264, 265 & 306. Psalm 25 quoted from the Sternhold and Hopkins version.
11 In 1594. Wright (1951) p. 306.
12 Wright (1951) pp. 273–4; Andrews (1959) p. 103.
13 Wright (1951) pp. 274–5.
14 Estimates of the size of the combined fleets vary from 73 to 78 ships. See Wright (1951) pp. 270, 275; Chaunu (1955) iii, 478 ff; BL Lansdowne 67 fos. 155, 161. These last two estimates have 33 ships from Mexico, 23 from the Spanish Main, 12 from Santo Domingo and 9 from Honduras.
15 Phillips (1986) pp. 157–8.
16 Cummins (1962) i, 20–1.
17 The following description rests on the letters of Navarro and Arteaga which are translated in Wright (1951) pp. 270–9 and on the deposition of Antonio de Ribero in BL Lansdowne 67 f. 155. These accounts have some discrepancies in dates and numbers.
18 Hannay (1897) p. 496.

CHAPTER SEVEN

1   Monson (1902–14) ii, 253.
2   For an excellent summary of intelligence relating to Spanish naval preparations see Wernham (1969) pp. 382–9 & Wernham (1980) pp. 401–2.
3   PRO SP94/3 f. 201. Letter to Burghley 3/13 December 1590.
4   Wernham (1984) pp. 448–9. Loomie (1963) pp. 61–5; Wernham (1980) p. 410. For a mass of letters and summaries of letters from Velazquez to the King in 1591 see AGS Estado 168. In a letter of 7 April 1591 N.S., he enclosed a paper from Chateaumartin who reported mainly on French affairs to the Spaniards while reporting the Spanish naval preparations in addition to French affairs to the English.
5   Wernham (1980) p. 405.
6   PRO SP12/238/133.
7   Ship movements from PRO SP12/239/102; see also SP12/238/154 — memorial to Lord Burghley 17 May 1591.
8   PRO SP12/239/52. Burghley to Howard, 21 June 1591.
9   See *CSPD* and *APC* for these orders and for a general discussion of government policy and action at this time see Wernham (1984) chs. 12–15.
10 *APC* 13 June 1591; HMC *Hatfield MSS* iv, 119–23; for details of the London privateers see BL Lansdowne 67 fos. 177–8; for the Queen's letter see PRO SP78/25 f. 6v.
11 Wernham (1969) p. 383.
12 AGS GA 341/293 & 294.
13 AGS GA 341/291 & 292. There is a reference to the dispatch of 'five or six carvels . . . to the Land's End of England' in the report of an Englishman who left Lisbon on 10 April. *CSPD* 25 April 1591, Dublin. I have however as yet found no reference to this landing in Cornwall in English sources. The activities of these Spanish ships probably account for the persistent rumour that the Scilly Isles were under threat.
14 AGS GA 323/1.
15 Monson (1902–14) i, 269–77; AGS GA 323/6; Fernández Duro (1898) iii, 79.
16 AGS GA 341/294; Wernham (1980) p. 404.

CHAPTER EIGHT

1   Falcão de Resende (1866) p. 138.
2   For the Spanish navy see Thompson (1976), ch. 7, and Casado Soto (1988).
3   Quoted by Wernham (1984) p. 130.
4   On the problems of English and Spanish tonnage measurements see Lander (1977); Martin (1977); Casado Soto (1988). For a list of sixty-nine ships built for the Spanish royal service between 1590 and 1600 see Monson (1902–14) iv, 73ff.
5   For a summary of English reports on shipbuilding see Wernham (1969) p. 386.
6   On Santa Cruz see *Revista General de Marina* for March 1988, a special issue to commemorate the quatercentenary of his death.
7   For information on Don Alonso see Fernández Duro (1876–81) v, 24, 274 and Monson (1902–14) i, 213, 245. See also his account of his service in AGS GA 321/43. For his letters see AGS GA 322/41, 42, 44, 45, 46; GA 323/33, 34, 35 etc.
8   Wernham (1984) p. 133; AGS GA 322/41.
9   AGS CM2aE 523; HMC *Hatfield MSS* iv, 103; AGS GA 324/54.
10 PRO SP78/25 f. 17.
11 Estimated rations needed for the fleet in AGS GA 341/62; Phillips (1986) pp. 163–77 & 241–4.
12 AGS GA 322/34; 327/48; Monson (1902–14) iv, 73–4.
13 GA 339/93; 324/54.
14 For a list of the fleet on 2/12 August see AGS GA 341/188 and for more information see 341/204 which lists the soldiers on each ship. Some of the small ships may have left the fleet by the time of the battle so it is quite possible that Tennyson's 'fifty-three' is

accurate. Most modern writers have underestimated the number of fighting ships in the fleet; e.g. Rowse (1937) p. 300 who said that only twenty of Bazán's fleet were fighting vessels & Wernham (1984) p. 298, fn. 22 'not more than a couple of dozen'. Fernández Duro (1898) iii, 79–80 said that there were fifty-five ships in Ferrol and the eight *felibotes* of D. Luis Coutinho which is correct, but four ships were left behind and only fifty-one of the fifty-five sailed.

15 '*Fortissimos . . .* ', Falcão de Resende p. 134; on Bertendona see especially Boxer (1969).
16 Raleigh p. 43; Falcão de Resende pp. 133–48; on the poem (which is in Castilian) and the poet see Ramalho (1969). I am indebted to my brother Tom Earle for this reference. For the soldiers in the fleet see GA AGS 341/204.
17 AGS GA 322/44.
18 Raleigh p. 42; the guns are listed in GA 341/188 and for an earlier muster see GA 341/183. For the guns on those ships which served in the Armada see Martin & Parker (1988) pp. 62–3.
19 For the guns of the *Revenge* see above pp. 42–3.
20 Gunpowder for each ship is listed in AGS GA 341/188. Maldonado in AGS GA 347/200.
21 Departure described in AGS GA 324/66, /84; Salazar translated in Phillips (1986) pp. 158–9.
22 PRO SP 94/4 f. 35. These are actually captured orders issued on 2/12 July. For orders issued by Bazán 'two hundred leagues from Spain' on 12/22 August see Bertendona MSS in Lilly Library, Bloomington, Indiana. See also AGS GA 322/44 for a summary of the orders in a letter written by Bazán on 18/28 June. He was to stay in the Azores until 5/15 October by which time all Indies ships should have arrived.
23 Salazar translated by Phillips (1986) p. 161.
24 Falcão de Resende p. 138. He actually says that they arrived at Terceira on the last day of August, i.e. 21 August O.S., but the official Spanish *relación* says 20/30 August.

CHAPTER NINE

1 Tennyson, p. 470.
2 For the history of the islands see Duncan (1972) and for a very good description during the period of this book see Linschoten (1598) pp. 178–92.
3 Cordeiro (1717) p. 491.
4 The central group had a strong Low Countries presence and was often called the Flemish Islands in contemporary maps.
5 Monson (1902–14) iii, 124.
6 AGS Estado 431/1 fo. 7. Order of Marqués de Santa Cruz, 1 August 1582 N.S. Tenison (1933) iv, 167–201.
7 Ferreira Drummond (1850) pp. 337–44.
8 A list of the guns in the islands is in AGS GA 328/183, together with Horbina's letter of 12 December 1591 N.S. about the defences of Flores and Corvo; Linschoten (1598) p. 186.
9 Linschoten (1598) p. 187. For a useful discussion of English policy regarding the Azores in the early 1580s see Scammell (1986) pp. 302–3.
10 Linschoten (1598) p. 193; Cordeiro (1717) p. 486; Monson (1902–14) i, 229–33; Hakluyt (1903–5) vii, 4–8.
11 Wright (1599) p. 4.
12 Gawdy (1906) pp. 62–3.
13 PRO SP 78/25 f. 6v; Linschoten (1598) p. 182; Monson (1902–14) ii, 254–6.
14 BL Lansdowne 67 fos. 150, 172v.
15 For the London privateers see Hakluyt (1903–5) vii, 56–62. For events in Flores see AGS GA 324/18; Cordeiro (1717) p. 486. Don Juan de Maldonado confirmed that it was Grenville who 'had robbed and burned the churches'. AGS GA 326/36.
16 Linschoten (1598) p. 192.
17 AGS GA 324/16.

18 Linschoten (1598) pp. 181–3, 186; Cordeiro (1717) pp. 484–5, 491–2.
19 BL Lansdowne 70 f. 229v; PRO SP12/240/101; Raleigh p. 41.
20 PRO SP12/238/152 letter dated 15 May; *APC* 18 May; Hakluyt (1903–5) vii, 56.
21 Raleigh p. 41 says 15 or 16 ships; Linschoten (1598) p. 193 says 16; Fernández Duro (1898) iii, 79 says 22 ships, as does the official Spanish *relación*.
22 Lloyd (1968) p. 45, quoted the remarks of a physician on board Lord Thomas Howard's ship in the 1596 expedition to Cadiz; Williamson (1935) p. 443 has a good description of 'rummaging'.
23 See Cordeiro (1717) p. 483 on the '*ancoradouro de navios*' south of Ponta Delgada; Callender (1919) p. 94 is inaccurate in saying that 'the only possible anchorage' was on the west of the island; on the wind see *relación* p. 484d; for the *atalayas* see Herrera (1612) p. 295.
24 PRO SP12/239/52; SP94/3 f. 201.
25 The sources disagree on the time when Myddelton arrived and on the date on which the battle started. Raleigh p. 41 says he arrived in the afternoon of the last day of August (i.e. 31) and that the Spanish fleet were in sight almost immediately. Monson (1902–14) i, 254 said the *Moonshine* arrived 'the very night' before the Spanish arrived. The Spanish *relación* says that the '*petachio*' arrived to give warning in the morning and all Spanish sources say it was 9 September N.S. (i.e. 30 August O.S.). I agree with Monson's editor, Oppenheim [Monson (1902–14) i, 262–3] and Callender (1919) p. 93 that Monson's account was more likely to be accurate since, if Raleigh had been right, Lord Thomas and the rest of the fleet would not have had time to get away. But it will be clear from the next chapter that he did not have much time, so I have accepted the Spanish evidence that Myddelton arrived in the morning. Raleigh might well have been confused since, as will be seen, two pinnaces arrived to give news — *Moonshine* and the pinnace which was cruising on the west of Flores which certainly did arrive almost immediately before the Spanish fleet was sighted. As for the date, it is unlikely that the Spanish commanders on the spot would have got it wrong. The battle of Flores therefore started on 30 August O.S. and ended on the 'last day of August' (i.e. 9–10 September N.S.).

CHAPTER TEN

1 García Lorca (1935), translated ibid. (1953).
2 In this and succeeding chapters, events from the Spanish point of view will rest mainly on the official *relación* and on Cabrera de Córdoba (1877) iii, 498–502, a contemporary history which draws very heavily on the *relación*. Events from the English point of view will rely mainly on Raleigh. For *Santo Tomás*, see Villavicencio's report in AGS GA 326/45.
3 AGS GA 341/272. Accounts of purchases in the islands.
4 Bertendona said that *San Andrés* had lost her fore-topmast (p. 470) and that other ships were lagging as well. He probably confused *San Andrés* with *San Pablo* (see above p. 120).
5 Maldonado, the *Veedor-General* of the fleet, is the only source to state the time of arrival at the island. GA 326/36.
6 Falcão de Resende (1866) p. 139.
7 García de Palacio (1587) pp. 120–5; Monson (1902–14) iv, 90; for a good idea of such preparations and the fighting positions taken up by soldiers at sea see the order of battle for *San Martín*, Santa Cruz's flagship in the 'sea-fight at the islands' of July 1582. AGS Estado 431/1.
8 Gawdy (1906) p. 62. English sources tend to ignore or play down the fact that Howard's fleet thought the approaching Spaniards were the treasure fleets. However, the Spanish sources say that this was so and I am inclined to believe them. The Spanish were coming from the south-west which is the direction from which the Indies fleets would be expected with an east wind blowing — i.e. tacking and not sailing directly east as they would normally do.
9 See, for example, Callender (1919) pp. 92–4; Corbett (1899) ii, 358–9 and Oppenheim in Monson (1902–14) i, 261–5.

10 Herrera (1612) p. 295. No one else gives this distance.
11 As reported to the Portuguese authorities by the captain of a Scottish ship which encountered the *Defiance* after the battle. AGS GA 326/2. Fuentes to the King, Lisbon, 5 October 1591.
12 Quotation from Linschoten (1598) p. 193.
13 Nearly all the Spanish sources say that the first shots were fired at five in the afternoon, but Raleigh has the battle starting at 'three of the clock in the afternoon'.
14 Bertendona p. 471.
15 Cabrera de Córdoba (1877) iii, 499.

CHAPTER ELEVEN

1 Opening quotation from Tennyson.
2 Herrera (1612) p. 295; Bertendona says there were 'three smaller ships' with the *Revenge* and Raleigh mentions one, the *George Noble* of London.
3 Blandy (1581) sig. 64, quoted by Evans (1972) p. xix.
4 Linschoten (1598) p. 92.
5 Bertendona p. 470; Falcão de Resende p. 139; Raleigh p. 42. In the rest of the description of the fight, the main sources will be Raleigh; *relación*; Bertendona; Cabrera de Córdoba and Falcão de Resende. Scraps of naval lore, etiquette, etc. have been taken from Monson (1902–14), Smith (1970), García de Palacios (1587), Hakluyt (1903–5) and similar works. Detailed references will not be given unless it seems necessary.
6 Hakluyt (1903–5) vi, 55; Smith (1970) p. 80.
7 For a discussion of this term see L.G.C.L., 'To spring one's luff', *MM* xxviii (1942) p. 78. In essence it means to alter course suddenly to windward.
8 Callender (1919) p. 95; the *relación* describes San Felipe and San Bernabe as the 'swiftest sailers'; Maldonado describes them as '*galeones nuevos y grandes beleros*' — AGS GA 326/36.
9 For the soldiers on *San Felipe* see AGS GA 341/204 and, for some details, Falcão de Resende p. 134. All further references to names and numbers of soldiers draw on these two documents.
10 Falcão de Resende p. 140.
11 AGS GA 326/21; AGS GA 338/167; sailors' pay from Phillips (1986) pp. 237–8.
12 The English translation of the official Spanish *relación* gives '*costado con costado*' as 'broadside to broadside' which is somewhat ambiguous. '*Costado*' means 'side'; '*andanada*' is the discharge of all the guns on one side of a ship. The word 'broadside' in English can of course have either of these meanings. Tenison (1933–60) viii, 484b, 484f.
13 Callender (1919) p. 95.
14 On problems of loading see Konstam (1988).
15 As pointed out a long time ago, though not for quite the same reasons, in Callender (1919) pp. 98–9.
16 For the powder left aboard see GA 326/36 & 44, letters from Maldonado and Urquiola to the King dated 10 & 11 October 1591. For the powder loaded in London see PRO SP12/238/51 and see above p. 44. The calculation of the consumption of powder by the lower-deck guns is based on the assumption that, at such close range, they used powder of three-quarters of the weight of the shot each time they fired. [See Sir John Davies in Monson (1902–14) iv, 34, fn.] In fact, they probably used rather more, reducing even further the number of times the guns were fired. [For details of powder consumption in different guns see Bourne (1587) pp. 66–70.] The weight of shot in the lower-deck guns was estimated as follows: 2 demi-cannon @ 30 lbs each; 10 culverins @ 17 lbs; 4 cannon-perriers @ 22 lbs; 4 demi-culverins @ 9 lbs — a total of 354 lbs, while the powder consumed was 20 barrels × 100 lbs = 2,000 lbs.
17 For interesting comments made in 1628 on the defence of royal ships in close fights see Harris (1983) p. 92. Smith (1970) p. 74. The description of fighting stations is based on Smith.
18 Hawkins (1933) p. 150.

19 Falcão de Resende p. 142. He uses the image of the bull for Grenville several times in the poem.

CHAPTER TWELVE

1 Opening quotation from Tennyson. Sunset in 40°N, 31°W on 30 August O.S./9 September N.S. is at 2024 GMT and sunrise is at 0740. I am grateful to Mrs Joy Hamblyn of HM Nautical Almanac Office for this information.
2 Phillips (1986) p. 140.
3 Smith (1970) p. 79; Cordeiro (1717) p. 484.
4 BL Lansdowne 70 f. 192v.
5 Linschoten (1598) p. 194; AGS GA 327/48.
6 Phillips (1986) p. 138; BL Lansdowne 67 f. 193.
7 For medicine in the navy see Keevil (1957). For a valuable insight into late sixteenth-century surgery see the writings of William Clowes in the selection by Poynter (1948). Clowes had seen much sea service and was surgeon of the *Ark Royal* in the defence against the Armada.
8 Monson (1902–14) iv, 57–8.
9 AGS GA 327/48.
10 This galleon is sometimes called *Asunción* and sometimes *Ascensión* in contemporary documents. I have called her *Asunción* as that was the name she bore in the campaign of 1588. See Martin & Parker (1988) p. 62.
11 Smith (1970) p. 79.
12 Callender (1919) p. 96.
13 PRO SP94/4 f. 92.
14 Clowes (1897) i, 496.
15 Raleigh.
16 Oppenheim (1896) pp. 352–5 — the case of Captain John Best of the *Adventure*. Accusations of cowardice were in fact very rare.
17 Linschoten (1598) p. 194; Gawdy (1906) pp. 53, 54, 57; final quotation from Tennyson.

CHAPTER THIRTEEN

1 Quoted and translated by Phillips (1986) pp. 159, 279.
2 Tennyson.
3 Hawkins (1933) p. 16; Raleigh p. 45; Camden (1688) p. 456.
4 Raleigh pp. 41, 44; Linschoten (1598) p. 193; *relación* p. 484f; Cabrera de Córdoba (1877) p. 501; Maldonado in AGS GA 326/36.
5 The following description draws almost entirely on Raleigh.
6 The official *relación* said that the Spaniards had 'many wounded but the dead numbered less than one hundred, including those lost in the *Asunción* who formed the majority'. This seems impossibly low after such an action. Raleigh (p. 47) said that 'well neere one thousand of the enemies' were slain and drowned which seems too high. Linschoten (1598) p. 193 puts the figure at 'above 400', which seems a fair enough compromise.
7 AGS GA 327/48. Bertendona to King, 4 November 1591.
8 Bertendona p. 470; Boxer (1969) p. 9.
9 Linschoten (1598) p. 193.
10 AGS GA 326/23. Bazán to King, 12 October 1591; Boxer (1969) pp. 10–11.
11 Quoted by Barrington (1956) p. 350.
12 Bertendona p. 470; Falcão de Resende p. 144.
13 Bertendona p. 472; AGS GA 326/26; *relación* p. 484f.
14 AGS GA 341/183 for the Ferrol list; GA 341/198, Lisbon, 17 December 1591. The weights are listed as if they were in quintals and Spanish *libras*, but it is clear that the guns could not have been weighed in Lisbon as a figure is not given for every gun. The weights must therefore have been taken from markings on the guns. Some English guns of

the period are engraved with their weight in English pounds and some in hundredweights, quarters and pounds and some do not record weight at all. So, what exactly the Spanish figures mean is a matter of conjecture. The data is reproduced below:

THE ARTILLERY WHICH WAS TAKEN FROM THE ENEMY ALMIRANTA

BRONZE GUNS	WEIGHT OF GUN (Quintals & *libras*)	WEIGHT OF BALL (*libras*)
One demi-culverin	22.15	9
Another demi-culverin	22.30	8
Another demi-culverin	24.02	7
Another demi-culverin	No weight numbers	8
A saker	11.91	5
Another saker	13.01	5
Another saker	17.00	5
Another saker	15.23	4
Another saker	15.11	4
Another saker	No weight numbers	4
Another saker	17.00	5
A demi-saker	8.21	2.5
Another demi-saker	8.23	2.5
A *pasamuro de camera*	No weight numbers	5
Another *pasamuro*	No weight numbers	5
Another *pasamuro*	No weight numbers	5
Another *pasamuro*	No weight numbers	5

Altogether seventeen guns

A summary at the end of the report describes the four *pasamuros* as *falconetes de cámara*, i.e. small breech-loading guns of the sort which would have been very busily engaged in the forecastle.

15 Urquiola's report in AGA GA 326/44 and see also Maldonado in GA 326/36. Both reports are dated 11 October N.S.
16 AGS GA 326/36; Raleigh p. 50; PRO SP12/240/97; see also SP78/27 f.75 — Palmer to ?Heneage 25 January/4 February 1592.
17 AGS GA 326/23, Bazán to King, 12 October; 327/48, Bertendona to King, 4 November; 327/13, Bazán to King, undated but sometime in November; Hawkins (1933) p. 16; PRO SP240/99 says the men of the *Revenge* were to have only five months' pay.
18 Boxer (1969) p. 10; AGS GA 326/61; GA 327/48.
19 *Relación* p. 484f; AGS GA 327/48; Linschoten (1598) p. 93; Gawdy (1906) p. 64 — letter from Lisbon Castle, 9 February 1592.
20 Linschoten (1598) p. 193. Linschoten said that Don Alonso himself would not visit Grenville on his sick-bed, but this is contradicted by Bazán in his *relación*.
21 Bertendona p. 471; Linschoten quoted in Rowse (1937) p. 315. The missing sentence is in the original Dutch, but was not known to English readers until the nineteenth century.

CHAPTER FOURTEEN

1 AGS GA 326/38. Maldonado to Esteban de Ybarra, Lisbon, 2/12 October 1591.
2 See the letters of Navarro and Arteaga translated in Wright (1951) pp. 270–79.
3 On the *junta* see Wright (1951) p. 272; Bazán in AGS GA 326/21 and Maldonado in GA 326/36.

4 For the account of the storm which follows, I have relied mainly on Maldonado in AGS GA 326/36; Bazán in GA 326/21; Urquiola in GA 326/44; Agustín de la Guerra in GA 326/57; Navarro and Arteaga in Wright (1951) pp. 270–9; Falcão de Resende pp. 145–7 and Linschoten (1598) pp. 194–5.

5 Bazán in AGS GA 326/29; Villavicencio in GA 326/45.

6 Falcão de Resende pp. 145–6.

7 Linschoten (1598) p. 194.

8 Ibid.

9 Monson (1902–14) i, 255.

10 Hakluyt (1903–5) vii, 56–62; AGS GA 343/55; 326/8; Falcão de Resende p. 147; see also BL Lansdowne 67 for the capture of *San Juan Baptista* of Santo Domingo.

11 Bertendona.

12 Monson (1902–14) i, 255; Raleigh p. 49; Linschoten (1598) pp. 194–5.

13 Chaunu (1955–9) iii, 478 ff.

14 Raleigh p. 49.

15 AGS GA 326/38.

16 Villavicencio in AGS GA 326/45; Urquiola in GA 326/44; Wright (1951) p. 272; PRO SP 94/4 fos. 64v & 71.

17 Maldonado in AGS GA 326/36; Bazán reported that only a foremast had been put in the *Revenge* in GA 326/21.

18 Linschoten (1598) p. 194; AGS GA 326/21. I must acknowledge my debt to my colleague Dr D. D. Hebb for this passage on the salvage of the guns. He was responsible for the discovery of most of the key documents.

19 AGS GA 326/202.

20 Linschoten (1598) p. 194; AGS GA 326/202.

21 AGA GA 626 — Consiglio de Guerra to King, 21 December 1604.

22 BL Add. 28, 439 fos. 123, 127v.

23 Ibid. fo. 123v.

CHAPTER FIFTEEN

1 Markham (1595).

2 David Hannay's introduction to Southey (1904) p. vii.

3 Raleigh's 1591 pamphlet has been reprinted many times. The edition used here is Hakluyt (1903–5) vii, 38–53.

4 Copies of the pamphlet were widely circulated in England and had crossed the Channel by December as we learn from a letter written to Burghley from Flushing. The writer, Sir R. Sidney, said it was very well written and he would impart it to everyone he knew. Wernham (1980) iii, 412. Luis Cabrera de Córdoba (1559–1623) was a *criado* of Philip II who was sent on several missions in Spain and abroad as well as being much admired as an historian by Cervantes among others. He clearly had access to documents in El Escorial which he used in his history. This circulated in manuscript before the first part, which covers the period up to 1583, was published in 1619. The second part, which includes his description of the last fight of the *Revenge* (pp. 498–502), was not published until 1877. For information on his career see Cabrera de Córdoba (1876) vol. i, pp. ix–xiv.

5 Arber (1871) xiv, 34.

6 Hawkins (1933) p. 16; Bacon (1629) pp. 33, 52–3; Evelyn (1674) p. 76.

7 Monson (1902–14) i, 254–5; ii, 263; Gorges (1905) xx, 103–4.

8 Linschoten (1598) p. 193; Laughton (1904) iii, 319.

9 *Biographia Britannica* (1750–7) p. 2289.

10 Froude (1852) pp. 62–3.

11 Kingsley (1939 ed.) pp. 20–1.

12 The date of Tennyson's poem in Lendell (1878) p. 233.

13 Leighton (1898) pp. vi, 28, 262. For a more recent, and well-researched, fictional account of the battle see Fullerton (1964).

14   Hannay (1897) p. 490.
15   E.g. Callender (1924) p. 77.
16   Southey (1904) p. viii; Hannay (1897) p. 493.
17   Corbett (1899) ii, 352; cf. Callender loc. cit.; Hannay (1898) p. 121.
18   Hannay (1897) p. 500; Black (1959) p. 413.
19   Stevenson (1887) p. 197; Corbett (1899) ii, 362; Fiennes (1917) p. 117.
20   Oppenheim (1896) pp. 352–5.

BIBLIOGRAPHY

T HIS LIST IS RESTRICTED to works referred to in the notes, where they are cited by surname of author or first word of anonymous works and the date of publication. If two dates are given, the more modern edition has been used. Place of publication is London unless otherwise stated.

Anderson, R.C., 'A list of the Royal Navy in 1590–1591', *MM* xlviii (1957)

Andrews, K.R., *Elizabethan Privateering: English privateering during the Spanish War, 1588–1603* (Cambridge, 1964)

Ibid, *English privateering voyages to the West Indies, 1588–1595* (Cambridge, 1959)

Ibid, 'The Elizabethan Seaman', *MM* lxviii (1982)

Arber, Edward (ed.), *The Last Fight of the Revenge at Sea* in *English Reprints* xiv (1871)

Bacon, Sir Francis, *Considerations touching a warre with Spaine* in *Certaine Miscellany Works* (ed. Rawley, 1629)

Barrington, Michael, 'The most high-spirited man on earth', *MM* xxxvi (1956)

Biographia Britannica (1750–57)

Black, J.B., *The Reign of Elizabeth, 1558–1603* (Oxford, 1959)

Blandy, William, *The Castle or Picture of Pollicy* (1581)

Boteler, Nathaniel, *Dialogues* (ed. W.G. Perrin, 1929)

Bourne, William, *The arte of shooting in great ordnaunce* (1587)

Boxer, C.R., 'The papers of Martín de Bertendona, a Basque Admiral of Spain's Golden Age', *Indiana University Bookman* x (1969)

Bushnell, G.H., *Sir Richard Grenville: the turbulent life and career of the hero of the little 'Revenge'* (1936)

Cabrera de Córdoba, Luis, *Filipe Segundo Rey de España* (first part, up to 1583) (Madrid, 1619, 1876)

Ibid., *Historia de Felipe II, Rey de España: segunda parte* (Madrid, 1877)

Callender, Sir Geoffrey, 'The Battle of Flores, 1591', *History* n.s. iv (1919)

Ibid., *The Naval Side of British History* (1924)

Camden, William, *The History of . . . Elizabeth* (1688)

Casado Soto, José Luiz, *Los barcos españoles del siglo* xvi *y la gran armada de 1588* (Madrid, 1988)

Chaunu, Pierre & Huguette, *Séville et l'Atlantique* 8 vols (Paris, 1955–9)

Chope, R.P., 'New light on Sir Richard Grenville', *Trans. of the Devon Association* (1917)

Clowes, W.L., *The Royal Navy: a History* vol. i (1897)

Corbett, Sir Julian, *Drake and the Tudor Navy* 2 vols (1899)

Ibid (ed.), *Fighting instructions, 1530–1816* (1905)

Ibid (ed.), *Papers relating to the Spanish War, 1585–7* (1898)

Cordeiro, Antonio, *Historia insulana das ilhas a Portugal sugeitas no Oceano Occidental* (Lisbon, 1717)

Cummins, J.S. (ed.), *The Travels and Controversies of Friar Domingo Navarrete, 1618–1686* (Cambridge, 1962)

Documentos para la historia . . . de El Escorial (Madrid, 1916)

Duncan, T. Bentley, *Atlantic Islands* (Chicago, 1972)

Evans, J.X., *The Works of Sir Roger Williams* (Oxford, 1972)

Evelyn, John, *Navigation and Commerce* (1674)

Falcão de Resende, Andrés, *Romance do succeso da armada que foi as Ilhas Terceiras no anno de 1591* in Fernández Duro (1866) pp. 133–147

Fernández-Armesto, Felipe, *The Spanish Armada: the experience of war in 1588* (Oxford, 1988)

Fernández de Navarrete, Martin, *Colección de Documentos* 32 vols (facsimile ed., Liechtenstein, 1971)

Fernández Duro, C., *Armada Española* vol. iii (Madrid, 1898)

Ibid. *La Conquista de las Azores en 1583* (Madrid, 1866)

Ibid. (ed.), *Disquisiciones náuticas* 6 vols (Madrid, 1876–81)

Ibid. *Don Pedro Enríquez de Azevedo, Conde de Fuentes* (Madrid, 1884)

Ferreira Drummond, Francisco, *Annaes da Ilha Terceira* 4 vols (Angra, 1850–64)

Fiennes, Gerard, *Sea Power and Freedom* (1917)

Froude, J.A., 'England's Forgotten Worthies', *Westminster Review* (July, 1852) also in *Short Studies on Great Subjects* (1867)

Fullerton, Alexander, *The Thunder and the Flame* (1964)

García de Palacio, Diego, *Instrucción náutica* (Mexico City, 1587, trans. J. Bankston, Bisbee, Arizona, 1986)

García Lorca, Federico, *Llanto por Ignacio Sánchez Mejías* (1935) in *Obras completas* (Madrid, 1955)

Ibid. *Lament for the Death of a Bullfighter and other poems* (trans. A.L. Lloyd, 1953)

Gawdy, Philip, *Letters* (ed. I.H. Jeayes, 1906)

Glasgow, T., 'English ships pictured on the Smerwick map 1580', *MM* lii (1966)

Ibid. 'The *Revenge* reviewed',· *MM* liii (1967)

Gorges, Sir Arthur, *A Larger Relation of the said Iland Voyage* in Samuel Purchas, *Purchas his Pilgrimes* (Glasgow, 1905) vol. xx

Hakluyt, Richard, *Principal Navigations* (Glasgow, 1903–5)

Hamilton, Earl J., *American Treasure and the Price Revolution in Spain, 1501–1650* (Cambridge, Mass., 1934)

Hannay, David, 'At Flores in the Azores', *New Review* xvi (1897)

Ibid. *A Short History of the Royal Navy, 1217 to 1688* (1898)

Haring, C.H., *Trade and Navigation between Spain and the Indies* (Cambridge, Mass, 1918)

Harland, John, *Seamanship in the age of sail* (1984)

Harris, G.G. (ed.), *Trinity House of Deptford; Transactions, 1609–35* (1983)

Hawkins, Sir Richard, *Observations* (ed. J.A. Williamson, 1933)

Herrera, Antonio de, *Historia General del Mundo ... del tiempo del señor Rey don Felipe II ... desde el año de 1585 hasta el de 1598* (Madrid, 1612)

Hoffman, Paul E., *The Spanish Crown and the Defence of the Caribbean, 1535–1585* (Baton Rouge, 1980)

Howard, Frank, *Sailing ships of war* (1979)

Hussey, R.D., 'Spanish reactions to foreign aggression in the Caribbean to about 1680', *Hispanic American Historical Review* ix (1929)

Keevil, J.J., *Medicine and the Navy*, vol. i, *1200–1649* (1957)

Kingsford, C.L., 'The taking of the *Madre de Dios*, Anno 1592', *Naval Miscellany* ii (NRS xl) (1912)

Kingsley, Charles, *Westward Ho!* (1855, 1939 ed.)

Kirsch, Peter, *The Galleon: the great ships of the Armada era* (1990)

Konstam, R.A., '16th-century naval tactics and gunnery', *IJNA* xvii (1988)

Lander, J.R., 'An assessment of the number, sizes, and types of English and Spanish ships mobilized for the Armada campaign', *MM* liii (1977)

Laughton, Sir J.K., 'The Elizabethan Naval War with Spain' in *Cambridge Modern History* vol. iii (Cambridge, 1904)

Leighton, Robert, *The Golden Galleon* (1898)

Lendell, Robert, 'Sir Richard Grenvile and the "Revenge"', *Geographical Magazine* v (1878)

Lewis, Michael, *Armada Guns* (1961)

Linschoten, Jan Huygen van, *Discours of Voyages into ye Easte and West Indies* (Eng. trans. William Phillip, 1598)

Lloyd, C.C., *The British Seaman* (1968)

Lockhart, James & Otte, Enrique, *Letters and People of the Spanish Indies* (Cambridge, 1976)

Lodge, Edmund, *Illustrations of British History* (1791)

Loomie, A.J., *The Spanish Elizabethans: the English exiles at the Court of Philip II* (1983)

Markham, Gervase, *The Most Honourable Tragedie of Sir Richard Grinvile, Kt.* (1595) in Arber, *English Reprints* xiv (1871)

Martin, Colin, 'Spanish Armada tonnages', *MM* lxiii (1977)

Martin, Colin & Parker, Geoffrey, *The Spanish Armada* (1988)

Monson, Sir William, *Naval Tracts* (ed. M. Oppenheim, 5 vols, 1902–14)

Norton, Robert, *The Gunner* (1628)

Oppenheim, M., *A History of the Administration of the Royal Navy* (1896)

Porreño, Balthasar, *Dichos y hechos del Señor Rey Don Philipe Segundo* (Cuenca, 1628)
Poynter, F.N.L. (ed.), *Selected Writings of William Clowes, 1544–1604* (1948)
Quinn, D.B. (ed.), *The Roanoke Voyages* 2 vols (1955)
Raleigh, Sir Walter, *A Report of the Truth of the Fight about the Isles of Açores* (1591) reprinted in Arber, *English Reprints* xiv (1871) and in Hakluyt (1903–5) vii, 38–53
Ibid., *Works* (Oxford, 1829)
Ramalho, Américo da Costa, 'O último combate de Sir Richard Grenville' in *Estudos sobre a época do Renascimento* (Coimbra, 1969)
Rodger, N.A.M., 'Elizabethan naval gunnery', *MM* lxi (1975)
Ibid., *The Wooden World: an anatomy of the Georgian navy* (1986)
Rodriguez Salgado, M.J. and others, *Armada, 1588–1988* (1988)
Rowse, A.L., *Sir Richard Grenville of the 'Revenge'* (1937)
Salazar, Eugenio de, 'Carta escrita al Licenciado Miranda de Ron, 1573' in *Cartas* (Madrid, 1866); also published in C. Fernández Duro, *Disquisiciones náuticas* ii, 178–200
Salisbury, W., 'The ships', *MM* lii (1966)
Scammell, G.V., 'The English in the Atlantic Islands, c. 1450–1650', *MM* lxxii (1986)
Shilton, Dorothy O., & Holworthy, R., *High Court of Admiralty Examinations, 1637–1638* (1932)
Smith, John, *A Sea Grammar* (ed. Kermit Goell, 1970)
Southey, Robert, *English Seamen: Hawkins, Greenville, Devereux, Raleigh* (1904)
Speed, John, *History of Great Britaine* (1688)
Stevenson, R.L., 'The English Admirals' in *Virginibus Puerisque* (2nd. ed. 1887)
Stone, Lawrence, *The Crisis of the Aristocracy, 1558–1641* (Oxford, 1965)
Stow, John, *Annales of England* (1605)
Strong, Roy, *The Cult of Elizabeth* (1977)
Tenison, E.M., *Elizabethan England* 14 vols (Leamington Spa, 1933–60)
Tennyson, Alfred, *The Revenge: a ballad of the fleet* in *Poems and Plays* (ed. T. Herbert Warren, Oxford, 1971)
Thomazi, Auguste Antoine, *Les flottes de l'or: Histoire des galions d'Espagne* (Paris, 1956)
Thompson, I.A.A., 'Spanish Armada guns', *MM* lxi (1975) pp. 355–71
Ibid., *War and Government in Hapsburg Spain, 1560–1620* (1976)
Waters, D.W., *The Art of Navigation in England in Elizabethan and Early Stuart Times* (1958)
Ibid., *The Elizabethan Navy and the Armada of Spain* (Greenwich, 1975)
Wernham, R.B., *After the Armada: Elizabethan England and the struggle for western Europe, 1588–1595* (Oxford, 1984)
Ibid., *The expedition of Sir John Norris and Sir Francis Drake to Spain and Portugal, 1589* (1988)
Ibid. (ed.), *List and Analysis of State Papers Foreign* vol. ii (1969); vol. iii (1980)
Williams, Neville, *The Sea Dogs: privateers, plunder and piracy in the Elizabethan Age* (1975)
Williams, Sir Roger, *Art of Warre* (1590) in Evans (1972)
Williamson, G.C., *George, Third Earl of Cumberland, 1558–1605* (Cambridge, 1920)
Williamson, J.A., *The Age of Drake* (1935)
Ibid., *Sir John Hawkins: the time and the man* (Oxford, 1927)
Ibid., 'Sir Richard Grenville' in Katharine Garvin (ed.), *The Great Tudors* (1935)
Wright, Edward, *The Voyage of the . . . Earle of Cumberland to the Azores* (1599)
Wright, Irene (ed.), *Further English Voyages to South America, 1583–1594* (1951)

INDEX

Entries in *italics* refer to ships